offense comes how does God want us to overcome that offense what is the right and proper attitude that we are to have in the eyes of God according to scripture. Here are some of the things that you might hear in the world to forgive someone is a sign of weakness the scripture say that forgiveness is a sign of greatness and true love. The world says never admit that you're wrong the word says admission of guilt causes us to receive mercy and grace from God the Bible tells us whoever tries to cover his sin he will not prosper but whoever forsakes them and confesses them will have mercy. The world says love is you never have to say that you're sorry. The Bible says that we are to ask forgiveness of the people that we offend when we are aware that we have offended them. The world says sometimes you have a right to hold a grudge the Bible says we are to forgive as God in Christ forgave us. how did he do that while we were still sinners he forgave us. even though it's unfair even though we were fighting against God rebelling against God in our nature even though we were still sinners Christ died for us. Ephesians 4:32 says we are to be tenderhearted forgiving one another even as God for Christ's sake has forgiven you. You

MATT 5: LOVE OUR ENEMIES

THE ROOTS OF CHARACTER
TEACHER'S MANUAL

A Character Workbook

by Wendell Smith

Generation Ministries of The City Church
Kirkland, Washington

This Edition Published by:
City Christian Publishing
9200 NE Fremont • Portland, Oregon 97220

Printed in the United States of America

City Christian Publishing is a ministry of City Bible Church and is dedicated to serving the local church and its leaders through the production and distribution of quality equipping resources. It is our prayer that these materials, proven in the context of the local church, will equip leaders in exalting the Lord and extending His kingdom.

For a free catalog of additional resources from City Christian Publishing, please call 1-800-777-6057 or visit our web site at *www.CityChristianPublishing.com*.

The Roots of Character – Teacher Edition
© Copyright 1994 by Wendell Smith
ISBN 1-886426-51-1

Teacher's Manual

Table of Contents

How To Use "The ROOTS of Character"

How To Use the ROOTS of Character

The "ROOTS of Character" Workbook is especially designed for use in the classroom environment and the new Teacher's Manual provides exciting new tools for just such a setting. The Christian Teacher is now equipped with a complete set for effectively teaching the dynamic concepts of Christian character. Over years of testing and exposure in various settings, "The ROOTS of Character" Workbook has proven to be an effective means of training young and old alike. And now with the use of this new Manual for Instructors, this teaching course becomes even more valuable. The "ROOTS of Character" Course is especially appropriate for the following:

    (1) Christian Education Program (Sunday School, Bible Studies, Adult Classes, Youth Groups, etc.)

    (2) Christian Schools

    (3) Bible Colleges

    (4) Discipleship Training

This course is also excellent for personal Bible study and self guided research. An individual can listen to the Audio-Cassette series and fill in the notes as if he were taking the course in a class. "ROOTS" can also be used in family settings for instruction of older children and getting them involved in discussion, Bible study, character development and edifying projects.

Once an Instructor has decided on the format for the course (in a classroom setting) a strategy can be mapped out to determine the best use of the material. For example, if a Teacher has a class scheduled once a week for an hour (Sunday School, Bible Study, etc.) the format might be considerably different than a class that meets twice a week. The design of the course would also vary depending on how long of a time period the class was to run. A High School or College semester, a Wednesday night Youth Meeting, a 9 week Adult class would all differ in approach and organized content. (See the section on "Course Outlines".)

Creative Use of "ROOTS"

The "Character Workbook" is designed in such a way so as to give Instructors and Leaders the flexibility to teach these principles in their own unique way in order to more aptly meet the specific needs of their group. However, in order to teach material designed and researched by someone else, it is necessary for the Teacher to master the material himself before instructing others.

It is our recommendation that the Teacher study the entire course before beginning to teach it to students. He should listen to each of the audio-cassettes and fill in any of the "notes" areas while, of course, jotting down his own ideas and insights. A thorough reading of the "Bible Search" sections will also enhance his preparation. Upon completion of his own personal study, he should be ready to prepare his own unique presentation of the material.

The following suggestions are given as creative aids for enhancing the presentation of the "ROOTS" course (and the younger the age group – the greater the need for creativity and variation of teaching methods):

1. Thoroughly study the material available to you and research any related areas that you might feel would add to the content.

2. Exercise flexibility in teaching the material the way you believe is best. Every ministry will have different emphases and you may want to enlarge on certain areas.

3. Make the material come alive with your own illustrations and personal experience. (Few illustrations were given on the audio-cassettes because of time limitations).

4. Use Creative Teaching Methods to enhance the material and increase attentiveness:
   (a) Illustrations and Stories
   (b) Chalkboard or Pictures
   (c) Overhead Transparencies (provided)
   (d) Color Slides
       (One pastor did an entire slide presentation on the "Roots of Character" for his congregation.)
   (e) Discussions, Panels, etc.
   (f) Dramatic Role Play
   (g) Creative Games
   (h) Bible Quiz
   (i) Original Songs or Poetry
   (k) Posters or Artwork

5. Organize the class with projects, assignments, quizzes, grading and the presentation of course certificates at the conclusion of the course.

Course Outlines

The following are sample structures for the course when implementing it in different settings. "ROOTS" can be organized and structured to meet the custom needs of any group according to the Teacher's desire, but these outlines are simply examples and suggestions.

9 MONTH COURSE*
(One Hour of Teaching a Week for
approximately nine months.)

Week No. #	TOPIC
1.	Introduction, Explain course, begin pp. 1-16
2.	Introduction, "How Character Is Formed," pp. 9-16
3.	"How Character Is Formed," pp. 9 – (Chart 4)
4.	"Principles of Character" pp. 19-22
5.	"Principles of Character" pp. 22-24
6.	"Principles of Character" pp. 24 – (Chart 6)
7.	"Principles of Character" pp. (Chart 7) – pg. 35 (+ Chart 9)
8.	Introduction to "BE-Attitudes" – "Overcoming Pride" – pp. 39, 40
9.	"Overcoming Pride"
10.	"Overcoming Pride" (Optional Session)
11.	"Overcoming Anger" pp. 53-55
12.	"Overcoming Anger" pp. 55-65
13.	"Overcoming Bitterness" pp. 67-69
14.	"Overcoming Bitterness" pp. 69-80
15.	"Overcoming Immorality" pp. 81-83
16.	"Overcoming Immorality" pp. 83-97
17.	"Overcoming Guilt" pp. 99-111
18.	"Overcoming Guilt" (Optional Session)
19.	Introduction to "DO-Actions" — "Developing Righteousness" pp. 115ff.
20.	"Developing Righteousness thru the Word" — pp. 115-127

21. "Developing Peace thru Prayer" — pp. 129-131
22. "Developing Peace thru Prayer" — pp. 131-144

23. "Developing Joy thru Life Witness" — pp. 145-147
24. "Developing Joy thru Life Witness" — pp. 147-156

25. (Make Up Session or Review)
26. "Righteousness" — pp. 157-166
27. "Righteousness" — pp. 166-168

28. Summary, Review, or Testing
(Presentation of Certificates)

A 9 month course seems to be too long for younger groups unless the teaching sessions are extremely creative and involve the students in motivational ways.

SEMESTER COURSES

An outline for the class being taught on a regular semester schedule could be developed by using the above outline but teaching two hours a week for approximately 14 weeks.

12 WEEK COURSE**

(One Hour of Teaching for twelve weeks)

This would be especially appropriate for an adult Education Class, a Youth Group Mini-Course or a Bible Study.

Week No. # TOPIC
1. "How Character Is Formed"
2. "Principles of Character" — pp. 19-25
3. "Principles of Character" — pp. 25-35
4. "Overcoming PRIDE"
5. "Overcoming ANGER"
6. "Overcoming BITTERNESS"
7. "Overcoming IMMORALITY"
8. "Overcoming GUILT"
9. "Developing Righteousness"
10. "Developing Peace"
11. "Developing Joy"
12. "Righteousness — The Tree of Life"

** *Bible Search sections and some details will have to be skimmed over or eliminated in order to cover the material this quickly.*

Many other Outline possibilities can, of course, be developed to suit the specific needs of the ministry in which you are involved.

The following are some creative titles for sessions correlating to the Workbook Sections. These would be good for use in Posters, Flyers, Church Bulletins or other promotional materials.

"How Character Is Formed"
> The Power of Grace
> Getting More Grace From God
> Reacting and Responding
> Developing Spiritual Muscles

"Principles of Character":
> Being and Doing
> Jesus' BE-Attitudes
> Two Trees
> Killing the Old-Man
> Achieving Self-Worth

"The BE-Attitudes":
> Victory Over Rebellion
> Kingdom Authority
> Spirit of Anti-Christ
> Power of Meekness
> Yielding To God
> Breaking the Bondage of Bitterness
> Letting Others Out of Jail
> God's Moral Standards
> The Price of Purity
> A Crystal Clear Conscience
> The Pillars of Conscience

"The DO-Actions":
> The Fruits of Character
> Righteousness, Peace and Joy
> Dynamics of Meditation
> Powerful Prayer
> Honest to God Prayer
> A Living Witness

"Righteousness — Tree of Life":
> Growing the Right Tree
> Putting It All Together
> The Rewards of Righteousness

Using The Audio Cassettes

The audio-cassette tapes are designed primarily for Teachers who are preparing to present "The ROOTS of Character" material as a course in a classroom setting. Although suitable for personal study, the cassettes are especially effective in the preparation process on the part of Instructors.

It is not recommended that the tapes be played to a class for teaching, as that approach lacks the "live" dynamics of interaction between teacher and student. (A small Bible Study group certainly might be an exception to this recommendation).

It is recommended that the Teacher use the audio-cassettes in the following manner:

(1) Listen to the tapes one side at a time and take time to meditate on the principles.
(2) Take notes in the Workbook section as the tapes are being played.
(3) Stop the tape periodically for extra notes, thoughts or meditation, and also when it is so recommended on the tape (usually cued by a musical segment).
(4) Relisten to the tape the second time without necessarily taking notes but to catch the overall impact of the concepts presented.
(5) Listen to all of the tapes and complete the entire Workbook, including "Bible Search" sections before attempting to teach it to a class of students. This will help the Teacher have a thorough understanding of the entire concept of the Book as well as a clear goal where he or she is taking the class.

The Audio-Cassettes in your notebook are in the following order:

Tape 1　Side 1　"How Character Is Formed"
　　　　Side 2　"Principles of Character"

Tape 2　Side 1　"The BE-Attitudes: Overcoming Pride"
　　　　Side 2　"The BE-Attitudes: Overcoming Anger"

Tape 3　Side 1　"The BE-Attitudes: Overccoming Bitterness"
　　　　Side 2　"The BE-Attitudes: Overcoming Immorality"

Tape 4　Side 1　"The BE-Attitudes: Overcoming Guilt"
　　　　Side 2　"The DO-Actions: Righteousness and The Word of God"

Tape 5　Side 1　"The DO-Actions: Peace and The Life of Prayer"
　　　　Side 2　"The DO-Actions: Joy and Being a Life Witness"

Tape 6　Side 1　"Righteousness: The Tree of Life"
　　　　　　　　(SONG: "Seasons of the Soul"
　　　　　　　　by Chris Christenson)

Using The Overhead Transparency Masters

Provided in this section of your Teacher's Manual are black and white "Masters" for making your own Overhead Transparency set for use in teaching. Visualization of the concepts involved in "The ROOTS of Character" can be a dynamic tool to enhance the impact of your instruction of these life-changing principles of Christian character.

These "Masters" can actually be incorporated for multiple use in your presentation of "The ROOTS of Character". The "Masters" can be used in the following ways:

(1) Overhead Transparencies
(2) Handouts for a Class
(3) Posters
(4) Promotional Materials
(5) Other creative ideas (perhaps even T-shirts in some cases!)

The "Masters" are made available for the free use of the local instructor. These can be used in any manner or any number of times without the permission of the Author or Publisher (*you have our permission*) with the exception of printing them for retail marketing or sale (an infringement of copyright law).

How To Produce an Overhead Transparency

The following are given as practical steps for the Teacher in producing actual transparencies from these "Masters":

STEP ONE: Purchase from a reputable company or office products supply, a box of **"Overhead Projection Transparencies"**. These can usually be purchased for under $50.00 per box of 100.

TWO STYLES:

(A) Transparencies for use with photocopy machines.

(B) Transparencies for use with Heat Transfer machines.

Consult sources in your area for more information. Many companies will produce these for you although it may be more expensive.

STEP TWO: Remove "Master" from Teacher's Manual Notebook and run through photocopy machine or heat transfer machine together with plastic transparency.

STEP THREE: 3 hole punch your transparencies and insert them into your Teacher's Manual Notebook with your "Masters". They are now ready for your use.

STEP FOUR: If desired, permanent ink colored pens can be used to add color to your transparencies for visual impact.

Teacher's Notes

My Thanks

To the first "character class" of Temple Christian High School who inspired me to work on this material . . .

To my friend, Ken Malmin, who encouraged and helped, and . . .

To my wife, Gini, whose special "ministry" to me can neither be measured nor expressed.

Dedication

This book is dedicated to my parents, Elwood "Woody" Sherman Smith and Dorothy Louise (Wilde) Smith, who gave to me and my brothers and sister the rich heritage of Christian character. There is no way to measure the profound effect of godly parents upon a person's life, but the results can be seen by the success of that person to reflect the character of Jesus Christ in life. I am proud to say that any reflections in my life are present because of my parent's love, patience, obedience, and dedication to God. To them I am eternally grateful for life, salvation and sound character, and to them I dedicate this book.

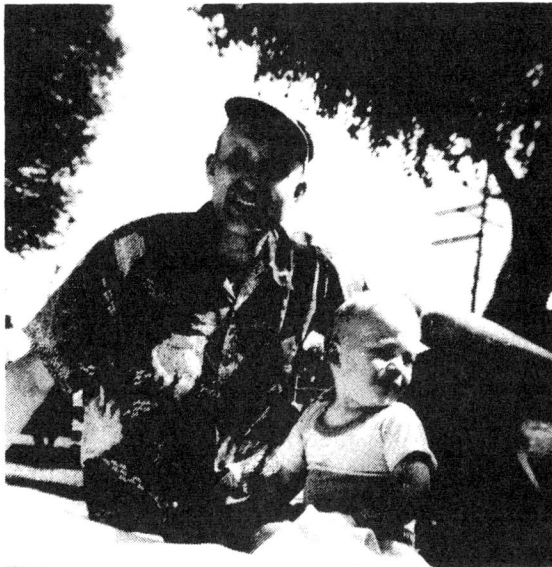

About a year before completion of this book, on my birthday, I received a card from my mother with the above picture, of my father and I, enclosed along with the following quotation . . .

> *"Like watching a seedling grow into a sturdy oak . . .*
> *so it is with a son."*
> *Love you lots*
> *"Mom"*

Unknown to her, this was a confirmation concerning this work and a blessing to me to consider again my rich heritage.

Wendell E. Smith

Table of Contents

All scripture references quoted from King James version.

Foreword

We are living today in the Church's greatest hour – an hour of spiritual restoration and renewal. God is moving throughout the earth in the lives of individuals and churches in tremendous manifestations of His sovereign power and glory. We are seeing before our eyes the returning of the Church to her original New Testament glory and pattern.

In the midst of this renewal and visitation there is a restoration of the supernatural gifts of the Holy Spirit. Many churches and groups today are experiencing these exciting vistas of the Holy Spirit and His power.

However, there is an increasing need among "charistmatic" and "pentecostal" groups for a return to the most necessary and basic of Christian virtues – the Fruit of the Spirit. With the increase of spiritual gifts, power and authority, there is a corresponding need for the balancing factor of Christ-like character in the Church.

Without the character and nature of Christ being manifested in the Body of Christ, there are grave dangers of extremism, deception, authority abuse and even self-destruction. I believe the "cry of the Spirit" in these days of revival and restoration is "balance the Church with character".

Wendell Smith, with his wife Gini, have labored with us here at Bible Temple for a number of years, working primarily with the youth of this Body. I believe one of the reasons for their success in bringing young people to maturity has been this very emphasis in their ministry on character.

I trust that this workbook will be of great benefit to the Body of Christ in moving us all closer to spiritual maturity and God's goal of "conforming" to the "image of Christ".

K.R. "Dick" Iverson
Pastor – Bible Temple
Portland, Oregon

Preface

When Jesus began his ministry on earth. His fame quickly spread throughout all Syria. No doubt the reason for His sudden rise to prominence was His miracles, His healings and His *mighty deeds*. On a particular occasion as the multitudes were following Him, we are told He drew aside into a mountain and sat down to teach. Undoubtedly, those following expected Him to do some mighty act or perform some miracle before their eyes. But instead, He began to teach them and to speak of *attitudes and inward desires*, of *"being" instead of "doing"*, of becoming a right person in the heart instead of attempting to perform right actions in the flesh. He spoke to those who listened about *fulfilling the Law*. The Law demanded "doing", whereas the Spirit of the Law, which Jesus proclaimed, encouraged first, "being".

This revelation of Jesus is the theme of this workbook, that "Being" precedes "Doing"! *What you are* ("being") will manifest itself in *what you do* ("doing"). Thus, when we speak of the basic *attitudes* given us in the "Sermon on the Mount," we can call them "BE"-attitudes. These are the *roots* of what God wants us to "BE". These are the makeup of the "inner man", the ROOTS OF CHARACTER, the "BE-Attitudes".

It has always been my personal conviction that Christians have forced themselves into the role of a hypocrite by trying to do certain right and accepted spiritual *activities*, when all along wrong *attitudes* in their own heart were condemning them, causing guilt, and robbing them of the very desire to engage in those activities.

Through an understanding of what we commonly call the "Beattitudes" in Matthew chapter five, we see that if a person will deal *first* with the *root attitudes* in his heart, then he will have corresponding inward desires to fulfill those right spiritual *actions*.

It is commonly agreed in Christian circles that a Christian should *read his Bible, pray to God,* and *witness to the unsaved*. We have, in many cases, taught our children and young people that an habitual practice of these three activities will produce progressing levels of Christian maturity. Practicing these activities will indeed produce stronger Christian character, but the truth is (as we will see in this workbook), that a person will not have the *inward desire* necessary to motivate himself in these activities until he has had some degree of victory and maturity in some basic *attitude* areas. This book deals with five root problem areas and gives teaching, scriptures, and steps of action in helping people begin the process of spiritual maturity.

Completion of this book and application of these steps will *not produce any magical results*, nor is this intended as a comprehensive, systematic study in counseling. Each person is uniquely different, and experiences vary in regard to serious needs in these areas. This book is not a "cure-all", and many root problems are far more complicated and complex than can be solved by a workbook of this nature. No man's book can ever adequately meet human need. There must always be personal, sensitive counseling with spiritual insight and discernment. There must always be an application of God's Word by His Holy Spirit, and in many cases there are needs for deep healing and deliverance.

But, a workbook of this sort is helpful in identifying problem areas in preparing our hearts for the work of God's Spirit.

Throughout the text you will find sections to fill in and pages on which to take notes. This teaching will be given to you by an instructor or can be received through the audio tapes provided for self study.

Some comments and notes which you record in your workbook may be of a personal nature. Therefore you may want to reserve the reading of your workbook to counselors, teachers, intimate friends or those in authority in your life.

I trust that your life will be affected for good through this study and that you will begin the sure and steady process of spiritual maturity.

May you be like a tree planted by a river of water, and may you bring forth the fruits of righteousness in your own time (Psalm 1).

God Bless You,

The Author

INTRODUCTION

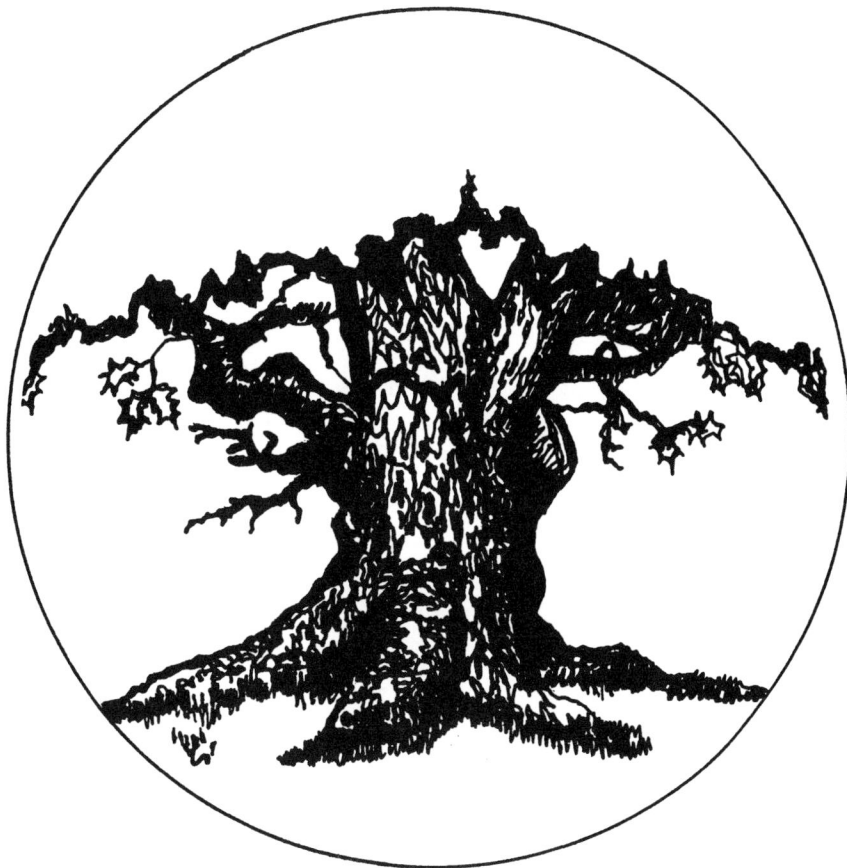

The Symbolism of the Tree

INTRODUCTION

The Bible tells us that a man's life is like a tree (Deuteronomy 20:19; Psalms 1; Psalms 52:8; Jeremiah 17:8; Psalms 92:12,13; Psalms 104:15,16; Proverbs 11:28,30; 12:3,12; Isaiah 61:3.)

God often uses the natural world to teach us great spiritual truths (Romans 1:20). The symbol of the tree is a tremendous and rich insight into what God wants man to be.

Our reason for choosing the tree as the symbol of this book is easily seen when one compares its basic structure with the life of man.

The leaves and fruit of the tree represent the *results* of a man's life or his *actions*.

The trunk of the tree represents a man's *character*.

And the roots of the tree represent the *basic attitudes* of a man's life.

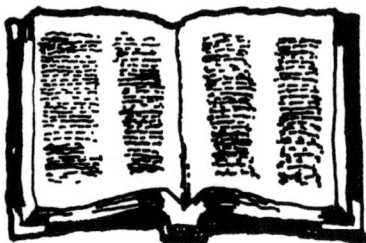

BIBLE SEARCH
on
The Tree

Look up the following scriptures on the "tree" as it is used in scripture and follow the proper instructions:

1. Look up *Deut. 20:19* and write out the portion of that verse given in parenthesis ( ):

   For the tree of the field is man's life. ☐

   Although this portion is here taken out of context in order to make a point, God gives us a little insight into the symbol of the "tree". (Complete the equation)

   "tree of the field" = "_man's life_" ☐

2. What is the godly man like, who is found in *Psalm 1* (see verse 3)?

   Like a tree planted by the rivers of water. ☐

3. Write out Psalm 52:8:

   But I am like a green olive tree in the house of God: I trust in the mercy of God forever and ever. ☐

4. Write out Psalm 92, verse 12, 13 and 14:

   12 _The righteous shall flourish like the palm tree: he shall grow like a cedar in Lebanon_ ☐

   13 _Those that be planted in the house of the Lord shall flourish in the courts of our God_ ☐

   14 _They shall still bring forth fruit in old age; they shall be fat and flourishing._ ☐

These verses show us that God Himself through His chosen man David, used the symbol of the tree to illustrate the life of a righteous man.

What two kinds of trees are found here?

(1) _palm_ ☐ (2) _Cedar_ ☐

5. **Write out:** *Proverbs 11:30:*

    The fruit of the righteous is a tree of life; and he that winneth souls is wise. ☐

    Proverbs 12:3:

    A man shall not be established by wickedness: but the root of the righteous shall not be moved. ☐

    Proverbs 12:2:

    The wicked desireth the net of evil men: but the root of the righteous yieldeth fruit. ☐

All these verses show us that a righteous man's life is like a fruitful tree.

6. **Write out** *Song of Solomon 2:3:*

    As the apple tree among the trees of the wood, so is my beloved among the sons. I sat down under his shadow with great delight, and his fruit was sweet to my taste. ☐

Again, in the poetry of love, God uses the symbol of the tree.

7. What does God desire to call those in Zion according to *Isaiah 61:3?*

"the _____trees_____ of _____righteousness_____"

"the _____planting_____of the Lord". ☐

8. Write out *Jeremiah 17:7,8:*

Blessed is the man that trusteth in the Lord, and whose hope the Lord is. For he shall be as a tree planted by the waters, and that spreadeth out her roots by the river, and shall not see when heat cometh, but her leaf shall be green; and shall not be careful in the year of drought, neither shall cease from yielding fruit.

_____ ☐

To what other scripture does this sound similar? _Ps. 92: 12-14_ ☐

9. Jesus warns us in the New Testament of false prophets. He uses the symbol of the tree. Look up Matthew 7:15-20, and answer the following questions:

• By what will you be able to recognize false prophets?

(vv. 16, 20) "by _____their_____ _____fruits_____" ☐

• A "good tree" produces what? (v. 17) "_____good_____ _____fruit_____". ☐

• A "corrupt tree" *cannot* produce what? (v. 18) "_____good_____ _____fruit_____". ☐

• What happens to trees that do not bring forth "good fruit"
(complete the equation:)

"false prophets" = "_____evil_____ _____fruit_____" ☐

page 4

10. In the book of the Revelation, chapter 11 verses 3 and 4, to whom does God give power for a special time?

"my _____ two _____ witnesses _____" ☐

And what does he call them in *verse 4?*

"the two _____ olive trees _____ ☐

and the two _____ Candlesticks _____" ☐

In all these scriptures, it is clearly seen that God uses the natural symbol of the tree to give us insight into the life of men.

As we study the roots of character in this workbook, may God reveal the beauty of His creation and His purposes to you as a "tree planted by the Lord".

Section One

HOW CHARACTER IS FORMED

HOW CHARACTER IS FORMED

1. What is the Definition of Character?

Webster's: *"moral excellence and firmness"*

Other: *the inner life of a man that will precisely reflect either the traits of the lower (sin) nature being influenced by the world, or the traits of the higher (divine) nature being influenced by the word of God.*

What are some scriptural synonyms for "character"?

divine nature
new man
inner man
spirit
heart
image of God (Christ)

2. God Wants to Form His "Character" Within Us

Fill in the blanks in the following scripture verses:

ROMANS 8:29 "For whom he did foreknow, *he* also did predestinate to be *conformed* to the *image* of his *son* "

ROMANS 12:2 "And be not conformed to this world, but be ye *transformed* by the *renewing* of your *mind* that ye may prove what is that good, and acceptable and perfect will of God."

GALATIANS 4:19 "My little children, of whom I travail in birth again until *Christ* be *formed* in you"

II PETER 1:4 "Whereby are given unto us exceeding great and precious promises: that by these ye might be *partakers* of the *divine nature*, having escaped corruption that is in the world through lust."

We can see from these scriptures that God wants to develop in us the _Character_ of _Christ_ .

This is the WILL of GOD, that we become like Christ or _Christ-like_ .

There is, however, *only one way* we can become like Jesus Christ, and that is if _God helps us_ .

If we try and become like Christ on our own strength we will simply be putting ourselves under the _Old Covenant_ and thereby be under the demands of the _law_ .

3. How does God form His Character in Us?

We find that since Jesus came, He gave man the opportunity of entering a New _Covenant_ . This was to be a _Covenant_ of _grace_ .

Look up and read:

☐ John 1:17
and
☐ Romans 10:4
and
☐ Romans 5:20
and
☐ II Timothy 1:9

What the LAW could only _demand_ under the Old Covenant, GRACE now _performs_ in us under the New Covenant.

Romans 11:6 says, "And if by *grace* (which is _God at work_ _within us_) then it is no more of *works* (which is _our own self-effort_)"

4. What is the Grace of God?

Webster's: _Unmerited, divine assistance given to man for his regeneration or sanctification._

Strong's: _The divine influence upon the heart and its reflection in the life._

Others:
(Bill Gothard)
An active force within us, giving us the desire and the power to do things God's way.

A PRACTICAL DEFINITION OF GRACE:

The God given desire and ability to accomplish God's will.

Here is scripture's amplification of the meaning of grace:

Write out Philippians 2:13: "_For it is God which worketh in you both to will and to do of his good pleasure._"

5. How does God's Grace affect our lives?

1. *We are saved by grace.*

"For by *grace* are ye saved through faith . . . *not* of *works* lest any man should boast." Eph. 2:8,9

(Also: Titus 2:11; Rom. 3:24; 5:2)

2. *We are given grace to help us in time of need.*

"Let us therefore come boldly unto the throne of *grace* that we may obtain mercy and find *grace* to help in time of need." Heb. 4:16

(Also: II Cor. 9:8; 12:9; Acts 4:33; Heb. 12:28)

3. *We are given supernatural gifts, abilities, and ministries through the grace of God.*

"Whereof I was made a minister, according to the gift of the *grace* of God given unto me by the effectual *working of his power*." Eph. 3:7

"But unto every one of us is given *grace* according to the measure of the *gift* of Christ." Eph. 4:7

The following are examples of God's *grace* at work in the lives of great men and women of the Bible: (You may want to read some of these accounts.)

☐ NOAH — Genesis 6:8

☐ JESUS — Luke 2:40

☐ APOSTLES — Acts 4:33

☐ BELIEVERS — Acts 11:23

☐ PAUL — I Corinthians 15:10

☐ TIMOTHY — II Timothy 2:1

How then will God's grace help us to develop the Character of Christ?

It is only by our proper ___response___ to God's grace that we are able to grow in our development of the Character of Christ.

Write out Hebrews 12:15 (as given by your Instructor): (Phillips)

" _Be careful that none of you fails to respond to the grace of God, for if he does there can spring up in him a bitter spirit which can poison the lives of many others_ "

6. How to Respond to God's Grace

1. There is a _wrong response to grace_ .

   "For there are certain men crept in unawares, who were before of old ordained to this condemnation, ungodly men, *turning the grace* of our God into lasciviousness." Jude 1:4

   (Also: Heb. 12:15; Rom. 6:1; Gal. 5:4; II Cor. 6:1; Heb. 10:29)

2. There is a _right response to grace_ .

   "I do not frustrate the grace of God . . . " Gal. 2:21

   (Also: II Tim. 2:1; I Cor. 15:10; II Cor. 1:12)

   What does Colossians 2:6 tell us? (Write it out)

   As ye have therefore received Christ Jesus the Lord, so walk ye in Him.

   How did you receive Christ as Lord?

   (see Eph. 2:8,9)

   by " _grace_ through _faith_ ".

   So Grace is _God's helping power within us_ .
   Faith is _our proper response to God's help_ .

SO THEN, WE ARE TO "WALK" IN CHRIST DAILY . . .

In every situation of life then, we are faced with the responsibility of _____ *responding* in the right way to *God's* *grace* . ☐

   * If we respond *in faith* , God
will *help* us and we will be *able* to do His will. ☐

   * If we fail to respond properly, God is not able to help us
and we will *fail* and His will
will not be accomplished . ☐

8. How Can We Receive More Grace?

1. **HUMBLE OURSELVES!**
   (James 4:6)

   > also I Peter 5:5
   >
   > God will give His "divine enablement"
   > to those who recognize that they need it.

2. **LEARN TO PRAY!**
   (Acts 4:31-33)

   > also Hebrews 4:16
   >
   > Because of Christ's sacrifice we now can
   > approach the throne of God through our prayers.

3. **RECEIVE GRACE DURING TROUBLE!**
   (Hebrews 4:16)

   > also II Corinthians 12:7-10
   >
   > When we are weak and powerless to
   > overcome a problem — God will strengthen
   > us by His grace.

HOW CHARACTER IS FORMED

React

Respond

(chart 1)

HOW CHARACTER IS FORMED

SITUATION

"And be ye not conformed to this world but be ye transformed by the renewing of your mind that ye may prove . . . the will of God."

Romans 12:2

(chart 2)

HOW CHARACTER IS FORMED

(chart 3)

HOW CHARACTER IS FORMED

7. Responding to God's Grace

SITUATION	(Man's Way) REACT	(God's Way) RESPOND
Someone Offends You	Hurt Grudges Pity Pout Defensive Anger Bitterness	Forgive, go to them, love, humble, put up with, pray
Faced with a seemingly impossible pressure situation	Run Worry Discouraged Give up Condemn Get depressed Lose health	Pray Trust Word Obey Counsel
Tempted to sin	Sin Rationalize Dwell on it	Run (n flee) from sin Pray Worship Self control Quote the word Get active for God
A Crisis Occurs	Blame Crumble Pity Breakdown Panic Hysteria Give up Attempt to work out on own strength	Praise Calm down - Call Lord - Call church

(chart 4)

Section Two

PRINCIPLES OF CHARACTER

PRINCIPLES OF CHARACTER

From Matthew 5

There are principles basic to the development of Character that we must understand if we are to see the Character of Christ formed in our lives. This section deals with those principles as they are given from the Bible, Matthew chapter five.

WRITE OUT Romans 12:2:

> " And be not conformed to this world: but be ye transformed by the renewing of your mind, that ye may prove what is that good, and acceptable, and perfect will of God. "

Write out another translation (as given by your instructor): (Phillips)

> Don't let the world squeeze you into its own mold, but let God remold your minds from within, so that you may prove in practice that the plan of God for you is good, meets all His demands and moves toward the goal of true maturity.

Being always precedes Doing

NOTES

AN APPLE TREE WILL BEAR *apples*.

A WALNUT TREE WILL BEAR *walnuts*.

A *orange* TREE WILL BEAR ORANGES.

A *fig* TREE WILL BEAR FIGS.

HERE'S WHAT YOU DO:	WHAT KIND OF CREATURE ARE YOU?
☐ FLY and LAY EGGS	*Bird*
☐ HOP, SWIM and CROAK	*Frog*
☐ GALLOP, EAT OATS and "NEIGH"	*Horse*
☐ EAT GRASS, GIVE MILK, "MOO"	*Cow*
☐ SWIM, BREATH THROUGH GILLS	*Fish*
☐ CRAWL, SHED SKIN, SWALLOW FOOD WHOLE	*Snake*

It is an *obvious* and *basic principle* of nature and all God's creation that the certain type of life of which a creature partakes will manifest itself in certain instictive behavior peculiar to that creature.

IN SIMPLE TERMS . . .

what you are

determines

what you do

Thus when we read the message of the "Sermon on the Mount" left to us by Jesus, we see that the emphasis He was placing on our lives was not on behavior but on attitudes.

OUR ATTITUDES DETERMINE OUR ACTIONS!

Scripture Text and Notes

"Ye have heard that it was said . . ."

"But I say unto you . . ."

MATTHEW 4:23 – 5:48

TEXT

23 And Jesus went about all Galilee, teaching in their synagogues, and preaching the gospel of the kingdom, and healing all manner of sickness and all manner of disease among the people. 24 And his fame went throughout all Syria: and they brought unto him all sick people that were taken with divers diseases and torments, and those which were possessed with devils, and those which were lunatic, and those that had the palsy; and he healed them. 25 And there followed him great multitudes of people from Galilee, and *from* Decapolis, and *from* Jerusalem, and *from* Judea, and *from* beyond Jordan.

5 And seeing the multitudes, he went up into a mountain: and when he was set, his disciples came unto him: 2 And he opened his mouth, and taught them, saying,

3 Blessed *are* the poor in spirit: for theirs is the kingdom of heaven. 4 Blessed *are* they that mourn: for they shall be comforted. 5 Blessed *are* the meek: for they shall inherit the earth. 6 Blessed *are* they which do hunger and thirst after righteousness: for they shall be filled. 7 Blessed *are* the merciful: for they shall obtain mercy. 8 Blessed *are* the pure in heart: for they shall see God. 9 Blessed *are* the peacemakers: for they shall be called the children of God. 10 Blessed *are* they which are persecuted for righteousness' sake: for theirs is the kingdom of heaven. 11 Blessed are ye, when *men* shall revile you, and persecute *you*, and shall say all manner of evil against you falsely, for my sake. 12 Rejoice, and be exceeding glad: for great *is* your reward in heaven: for so persecuted they the prophets which were before you.

page 22

NOTES

The reason for Jesus' fame was his actions (deeds) but when he sets his disciples down, he teaches them about ATTITUDES!

5 Attitudes (BE-Attitudes):
1. Poor in Spirit - humble
2. Meek — trusting
3. Merciful - forgiving
4. Pure in heart - pure
5. Peace makers - clear conscience

3 Actions (DO-Actions):

1. Mourn - Prayer
2. Hunger - Word
3. Persecuted for - Witness righteousness sake

TEXT

¹³ Ye are the salt of the earth: but if the salt have lost his savour, wherewith shall it be salted? It is thenceforth good for nothing, but to be cast out, and to be trodden under foot of men.   ¹⁴ Ye are the light of the world. A city that is set on a hill cannot be hid.   ¹⁵ Neither do men light a candle, and put it under a bushel, but on a candlestick; and it giveth light unto all that are in the house.

¹⁶ Let your light so shine before men, that they may see your good works, and glorify your Father which is in heaven.

¹⁷ Think not that I am come to destroy the law, or the prophets: I am not come to destroy, but to fulfil.   ¹⁸For verily I say unto you, Till heaven and earth pass, one jot or one tittle shall in no wise pass from the law, till all be fulfilled.   ¹⁹ Whosoever therefore shall break one of these least commandments, and shall teach men so, he shall be called the least in the kingdom of heaven: but whosoever shall do and teach *them*, the same shall be called great in the kingdom of heaven.   ²⁰ For I say unto you, That except your righteousness shall exceed *the righteousness* of the scribes and Pharisees, ye shall in no case enter into the kingdom of heaven.

²¹ Ye have heard that it was said by them of old time, Thou shalt not kill; and whosoever shall kill shall be in danger of the judgment: ²² But I say unto you, That whosoever is angry with his brother without a cause shall be in danger of the judgment: and whosoever shall say to his brother, Raca, shall be in danger of the council: but whosoever shall say, Thou fool, shall be in danger of hell fire.   ²³ Therefore if thou bring thy gift to the altar, and there rememberest that thy brother hath aught against thee;   ²⁴ Leave there thy gift before the altar, and go thy way; first be reconciled to thy brother, and then come and offer thy gift.   ²⁵ Agree with thine adversary quickly, while thou art in the way with him; lest at any time the adversary deliver thee to the judge, and the judge deliver thee to the officer, and thou be cast into prison.   ²⁶ Verily I say unto thee, Thou shalt by no means come out thence, till thou hast paid the uttermost farthing.

²⁷ Ye have heard that it was said by them of old time, Thou shalt not commit adultery: ²⁸ But I say unto you, That whosoever looketh on a woman to lust after her hath committed adultery with her already in his heart.   ²⁹ And if thy right eye offend thee, pluck it out, and cast *it* from thee: for it is profitable for thee that one of thy members should perish, and not *that* thy whole body should be cast into hell.   ³⁰ And if thy right hand offend thee, cut it off, and cast *it* from thee: for it is profitable for thee that one of thy members should perish, and not *that* thy whole body should be cast into hell.   ³¹ It hath been said, Whosoever shall put away his wife, let him give her a writing of divorcement: ³² But I say unto you, That whosoever shall put away his wife, saving for the cause of fornication, causeth her to commit adultery: and whosoever shall marry her that is divorced committeth adultery.

NOTES

"Salt":
1. Preservative
2. Flavor
3. Influence
4. Value

"Light":
The oil on the inside of the lamp burns brightly in flame on the outside.

Jesus came to fill the LAW (external) full of meaning (internal).

How To Exceed In Righteousness:

1. "Blessed are the Meek"

Law	Fulfillment
Don't kill (law deals with outward actions!)	Don't be angry (fulfillment deals with inward attitudes!)

2. "Blessed are the Pure in Heart"

Law	Fulfillment
Don't commit adultery	Don't lust

³³ Again, ye have heard that it hath been said by them of old time, Thou shalt not forswear thyself, but shalt perform unto the Lord thine oaths: ³⁴ But I say unto you, Swear not at all; neither by heaven; for it is God's throne: ³⁵ Nor by the earth; for it is his footstool: neither by Jerusalem; for it is the city of the great King. ³⁶ Neither shalt thou swear by thy head, because thou canst not make one hair white or black. ³⁷ But let your communication be, Yea, yea; Nay, nay: for whatsoever is more than these cometh of evil.

3. "Blessed are the poor in Spirit"

Law	Fulfillment
Don't swear in vain	Don't swear at all (Don't be proud)

³⁸ Ye have heard that it hath been said, An eye for an eye, and a tooth for a tooth: ³⁹ But I say unto you, That ye resist not evil: but whosoever shall smite thee on thy right cheek, turn to him the other also. ⁴⁰ And if any man will sue thee at the law, and take away thy coat, let him have *thy* cloak also. ⁴¹ And whosoever shall compel thee to go a mile, go with him twain. ⁴² Give to him that asketh thee, and from him that would borrow of thee turn not thou away.

4. "Blessed are the Merciful"

Law	Fulfillment
An eye for an eye	Don't seek revenge (Forgive!)

⁴³ Ye have heard that it hath been said, Thou shalt love thy neighbour, and hate thine enemy. ⁴⁴ But I say unto you, Love your enemies, bless them that curse you, do good to them that hate you, and pray for them which despitefully use you, and persecute you; ⁴⁵ That ye may be the children of your Father which is in heaven: for he maketh his sun to rise on the evil and on the good, and sendeth rain on the just and on the unjust. ⁴⁶ For if ye love them which love you, what reward have ye? do not even the publicans the same? ⁴⁷ And if ye salute your brethren only, what do ye more *than others?* do not even the publicans so?

5. "Blessed are the peacemakers..."

Law	Fulfillment
Hate your enemy	Love, bless, do good and pray for people.

⁴⁸ Be ye therefore perfect, even as your Father which is in heaven is perfect.

"BE" perfect

God does not demand perfect actions, but He asks for perfect Attitudes!

Amplification of Romans 12:2

"Ye have heard that it was said . . ."

"But I say unto you . . ."

What the world tries to do

Conform

The BASIC APPEAL is:

__External__

What God does

Transform

The BASIC APPEAL is:

__Internal__

MEANS THE WORLD USES:

TV
Radio
Advertising
Movies
Style
Fads and Fashions
Education
Books
Newspaper
Music
Money
Business Success
Food

Lk. 21:26   I Tim 6:6-10
I Cor. 7:31   Mt. 16:26
Mt. 6:28-30   Mt. 7:31
I Pet. 3:3   Lk. 12:15

MEANS GOD USES:

Word of God
Prayer
Worship
Fellowship
Holy Spirit
Authority
Godly Music
Trials
Tests
Teaching
Preaching
Counsel
Christian Education

II Tim. 3:16
II Cor. 3:18
II Cor. 4:17
I Pet. 1:6-7

(chart 5)

The Typical Christian Dilemma

The typical Christian goes to a Counselor to resolve some basic conflicts in his life.

Parents of a teenager are concerned that she is not growing spiritually as she should.

A Pastor constantly exhorts his congregation to engage in activities that will enhance their spiritual life.

A Christian School Teacher is concerned about the spiritual apathy of some of his students.

In each case, we could all write out the "doctor's" prescription for remedy and spiritual "health" (or so we think we could). If we were to ask you to recommend 3 things that every "typical" christian should do to improve their spiritual state, what would you say?

Whether counselor, parent, pastor or teacher, all of us have, at times, advised other believers to engage in the following 3 activities:

1. Read your Bible
2. Pray More
3. Witness

But the truth is, we have frustrated ourselves and others by trying to deal with our *actions* before some basic heart *attitudes* were corrected. If we would first repent of our rebellion, our anger, our hurts, our wrong desires and clear our conscience, we would discover a new and dynamic inward strength to perform those things that would increase that same strength and produce greater levels of spiritual growth.

RESOLVED:

"You can never _____do_____ what God wants you to _____do_____,

until you first _____be_____ what He wants you to _____be_____."

Root Problems in the BE-Attitudes

MATTHEW 5:1-12

	SCRIPTURE	ATTITUDE	MEANING	OPPOSITE Root Problem
"BE" ATTITUDES	1 Blessed are the POOR IN SPIRIT	Humble	Submissiveness Obedience Trust and dependance upon God	Pride
	2 Blessed are the MEEK	Trusting	Yielding to the desires of others and not striving for position or possession.	Anger
	3 Blessed are the MERCIFUL	Forgiving	Having mercy toward others and their offences	Bitterness
	4 Blessed are the PURE IN HEART	Morally Pure	Virtue and holiness of thoughts and desires	Moral Impurity
	5 Blessed are the PEACEMAKERS	Clear Conscience	Peace of mind before God and man	Guilt
	SCRIPTURE	ACTION	MEANING	OPPOSITE
"DO" ACTIONS	Blessed are those who HUNGER AND THIRST AFTER RIGHTEOUSNESS	Seeking God	Getting to know God through His word Desires God's word	Apathy
	Blessed are those who MOURN	Sensitivity to God	Pouring your heart out to God in prayer Life of prayer	Anxiety
	Blessed are those who are PERSECUTED FOR RIGHTEOUSNESS' SAKE	Living for God	Being a life witness of the reality of Jesus Christ.	Fear

(chart 6)

The Real "Roots" of Character

**TREE OF
LIFE**

**TREE OF
SIN AND DEATH**

(chart 7)

THE "OLD MAN"

"The truth is in Jesus: that ye *put off* concerning the former conversation the *old man*, which is corrupt according to the deceitful lusts."

WHAT IS THE "OLD MAN"?

The nature of man with which he is born, that has the tendency to sin — selfishness, pride, rebellion against God and His laws.

WHERE DID THE "OLD MAN" ORIGINATE?

(See Genesis 2:15-17; 3:1-8;

Ephesians 4:17-22; Colossians 3:5-9)

SOME EVIDENCES OF THE "OLD MAN":

□ ADULTERY

□ SEXUAL IMMORALITY

□ IMPURITY OF MIND

□ SENSUALITY

□ WORSHIP OF FALSE GODS

□ WITCHCRAFT

□ HATRED

□ JEALOUSY

□ BAD TEMPER

□ ANGER

□ STRIFE

□ FEAR

□ RIVALRY

□ SELFISHNESS

□ DRUNKENNESS

□ ENVY

□ PARTY SPIRIT

□ ARGUING

□ ORGIES

□ LUST

□ HOMOSEXUALITY

□ SEXUAL PERVERSION

□ MURDER

□ SCOFFING

□ STEALING

□ LIEING

□ CONCEIT

□ DECEIT

□ GREED

□ CHEATING

□ REBELLION

□ LAZINESS

□ GOSSIP

□ COVETING

□ BOASTING

□ DOUBT

How can I get rid of the "Old Man"?

God's desire for every man is to become a "New Man", and He has made a gracious provision for just that through Jesus Christ. Nearly 2000 years ago, Jesus Christ died on the cross of Calvary. When He did, He nailed our sins to the tree by taking them upon Himself and thereby destroying the "Old Man" in His own flesh. It was by the supreme sacrifice of His own life that we are now able to become God's "New Man".

Write out Romans 6:6: _Knowing this, that our old man is crucified with him, that the body of sin might be destroyed, that henceforth we should not serve sin._

There are basically 3 STEPS to getting rid of the "Old Man".

1. PUT OFF THE OLD MAN

Write out Ephesians 4:22:

That ye put off concerning the former conversation the old man, which is corrupt according to the deceitful lusts

Write out Colossians 3:8,9:

But now ye also put off all these; anger, wrath, malice, blasphemy, filthy communication out of your mouth. Lie not one to another, seeing that ye have put off the old man with his deeds.

page 28

2. BE RENEWED IN YOUR MIND

Write out Ephesians 4:23:

And be renewed in the
spirit of your mind.

Write out Romans 12:2:

And be not conformed to this world: but be
ye transformed by the renewing of your mind,
that ye may prove what is that good, and
acceptable, and perfect will of God.

3. PUT ON THE "NEW MAN"

Write out Romans 13:14: But put ye on the
Lord Jesus Christ, and make not provision
for the flesh, to fulfil the lusts
thereof.

Write out Ephesians 4:24:

And that ye put on the new man,
after which God is created in
righteousness and true holiness.

Write out Colossians 3:10:

And have put on the new man,
which is renewed in knowledge in
knowledge after the image of him
that created him.

THE "NEW MAN"

"The truth is in Jesus: that ye put on the new man, which after God is created in righteousness and true holiness."

WHAT IS THE "NEW MAN"?

It is the new nature imparted to man when he is born again. A divine nature of love, righteousness and submission to God.

WHERE DID THE "NEW MAN" ORIGINATE?

(See Corinthians 5:17; Romans 6:3-11;
Galatians 3:27)

SOME EVIDENCES OF THE "NEW MAN":

□ LOVE   □ GODLINESS   □ PURITY

□ JOY   □ BROTHERLY KINDNESS   □ MERCY

□ PEACE   □ DILIGENCE   □ CONTENTMENT

□ PATIENCE   □ COMPASSION   □ COURAGE

□ GENTLENESS   □ WISDOM   □ LOYALTY

□ GOODNESS   □ UNDERSTANDING   □ EDIFYING WORDS

□ MEEKNESS   □ OBEDIENCE   □ HONESTY

□ FAITH   □ TRUST   □ INTEGRITY

□ TEMPERANCE   □ KINDNESS   □ GENEROSITY

□ VIRTUE   □ RIGHTEOUSNESS

□ KNOWLEDGE   □ HOLINESS

GOD'S DESIGN FOR A NEW MAN

The Restoration of Man

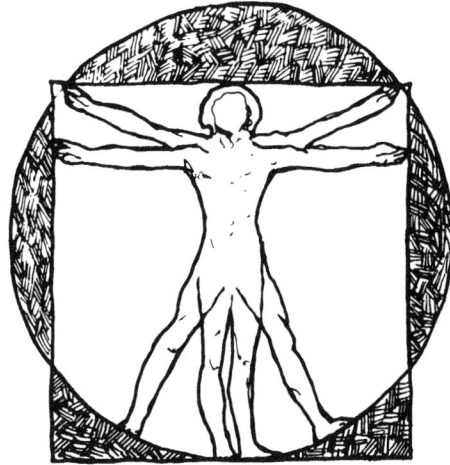

**GOD'S MAN
CREATED**
(Gen. 2:7-9, 15-17)

Tree of Knowledge
of Good and Evil

Tree of Life

GARDEN of EDEN

GOD'S "NEW MAN" RESTORED

MAN DIES

"Old Man" produced
through sin
(Gen. 3:1-24)

to Eternal
Life
(Rev. 22:1)

JESUS DIES
Christ Jesus, the God-Man
dies for the "Old Man" *(Rom. 5:8 / 6:6)*

"NEW MAN" CREATED
through Grace
(Eph. 4:24)

(chart 8)

Manifestations of the "New Man"

1. THE ACHIEVING OF TRUE SELF-ESTEEM

Our attitude toward ourself, which makes up our self-image, is produced by people, experiences and our natural abilities and appearance. Depending on the success or failure of these relationships, and the attitude we develop toward the way we are, we will either become stable, reject ourself, or become overly concerned with ourself resulting in pride and conceit, etc. The following relationships and areas of our life affect our sense of self-esteem and our self-image:

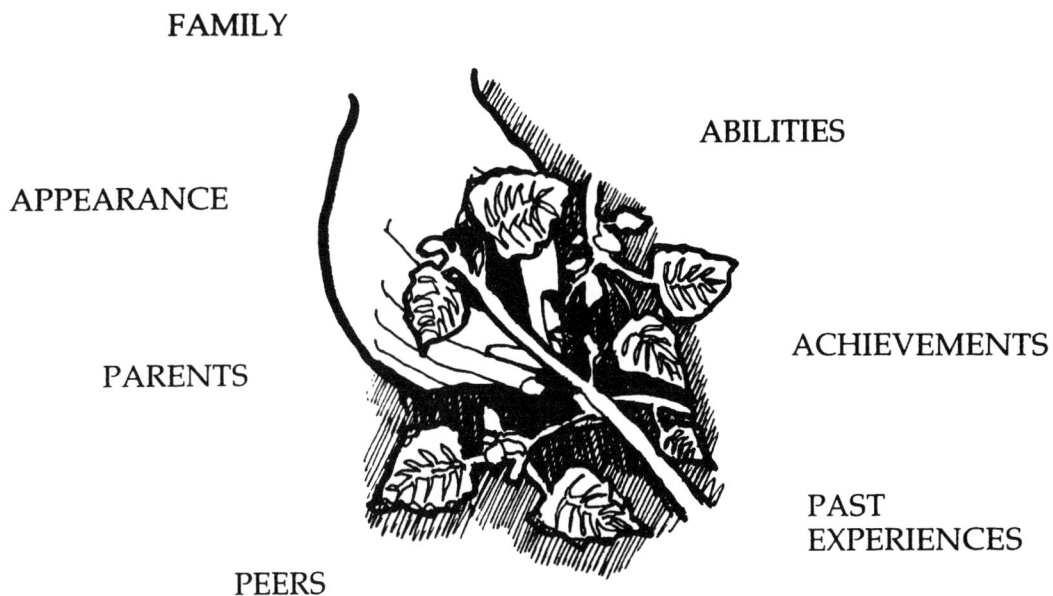

FAMILY

ABILITIES

APPEARANCE

ACHIEVEMENTS

PARENTS

PAST
EXPERIENCES

PEERS

God does not want our attitude toward ourself to be wrong or out of proportion in any way. It is only through becoming a "NEW MAN" in Jesus Christ and seeing ourself in the light of Scripture that true Self-Worth can be achieved.

STEPS TO ACHIEVING TRUE CHRISTIAN SELF ESTEEM

God created every man and woman and it is only by total commitment to the Creator's design and universal principles that each man and woman can come to know a complete fulfillment in life.

A. YOU MUST BE "BORN AGAIN"!
(See: *John 3:1-21*
II Cor. 5:17)

When you are "born-again" into the Kingdom of God, you become a new person inwardly with a new life and any outward "defects" become subordinate to our new "spiritual man."

B. YOU MUST BELIEVE THE WORD OF GOD!
(See: *Romans 10:10*
Phil. 3:13,14)

God looks at your heart (I Sam. 16:7) and He wants to give you a new perspective of yourself from His world. (See Eph. 1:3-6; Psalm 139; etc.)

C. YOU MUST LIVE IN OBEDIENCE TO THE WORD OF GOD!
(See: *I Peter 1:22*)

We must continue to live our daily lives in the revelation that we are God's children, that He loves us and that He accepts us, and that we have been chosen by Him to fulfil our destiny.

2. THE DEVELOPING OF POWERFUL, GODLY HABITS

"The truth is in Jesus: that ye *PUT OFF* concerning the former conversation the old man, which is corrupt according to the deceitful lusts; And be renewed in the spirit of your mind; And that ye *PUT ON* the new man, which after God is created in righteousness and true holiness."

Ephesians 4:21-24

After discussing each basic root problem area in the chapters following, there will be steps of action given as to how to practically overcome the basic problem.

A very key principle in scripture in "overcoming evil" is overcoming it "with good". (Romans 12:21)

Write out the following scriptures and this will be further illustrated:

Galatians 5:16 _This I say then, walk in the Spirit, and ye shall not fulfil the lust of the flesh._

Romans 13:14 _But put ye on the Lord Jesus Christ, and make not provision for the flesh, to fulfil the lusts thereof._

Romans 6:13 _Neither yield ye your members as instruments of unrighteousness unto sin: but yield yourselves unto God, as those that are alive from the dead, and your members as instruments of righteousness unto God._

Romans 8:2 *For the law of the spirit of life in Christ Jesus hath made me free from the law of sin and death.*

Ephesians 4:28 *Let him that stole steal no more: but rather let him labour, working with his hands the thing which is good, that he may have to give to him that needeth.*

Ephesians 4:29 *Let no corrupt communication proceed out of your mouth, but that which is good to the use of edifying, that it may minister grace unto the hearers.*

Deuteronomy 6:23 *And he brought us out ... that he might bring us in ...*

Romans 13:12 *The night is far spent, the day is at hand: let us therefore cast off the works of darkness and let us put on the armour of light.*

Colossians 3:9,10 *Lie not one to another, seeing that ye have put off the old man with his deeds; and have put on the new man, which is renewed in knowledge after the image of him that created him.*
(See also verses 8-14)

3. THE TRANSFORMING OF THE MIND

"Be ye transformed by the renewing of your mind."   Romans 12:2

"Be renewed in the spirit of your mind."

"Let this mind be in you, which was also in Christ Jesus."   Phil. 2:5

"Arm yourselves likewise with the same mind."   I Peter 4:1

If a person can renew his mind and his thought patterns, he can influence and control his actions, his habits and his ultimate destiny!

SOW A THOUGHT
   . . . *REAP AN ACT,*
SOW AN ACT
   . . . *REAP A HABIT,*
SOW A HABIT
   . . . *REAP A CHARACTER,*
SOW A CHARACTER
   . . . *REAP A DESTINY!*

LIFE

The RIGHTEOUS
The GODLY
The SAINT

DEATH

The UNRIGHTEOUS
The UNGODLY
The SINNER

DESTINY

C H A R A C T E R

H A B I T S

RIGHTEOUSNESS

WICKEDNESS

A C T I O N S

FRUIT of the SPIRIT

Gal. 5:22,23

WORKS of the FLESH

Gal. 5:19-21

T H O U G H T S

BASED ON
WORD
OF GOD

BASED ON
WORLD
PHILOSOPHY

CLEAR CONSCIENCE

GUILT

PURE   FORGIVING

TRUSTING

HUMILITY

MORALLY   BITTER

IMPURE

ANGER

PRIDE

A T T I T U D E S

N A T U R E

NEW MAN

OLD MAN

(chart 9)

Section Three

THE BE-ATTITUDES
The Roots of Character

ROOT 1 AREA

DEVELOPING A HUMBLE ATTITUDE

Overcoming Pride

*"God resisteth the proud
but giveth grace to the humble."*
James 4:6

THE ROOT PROBLEM OF THE WORLD

Man's basic nature is in rebellion against God. His natural inclination is to rule over his own life, heap up treasure for himself, glory in his own strength and ability and trust in his own wisdom. Left to himself, he is foolish, self-centered and proud. THIS IS *THE* BASIC ROOT OF ALL MAN'S PROBLEMS

PRACTICAL EVIDENCES OF THE ROOT OF PRIDE:

- Independent spirit – not looking to God or others for help.

- Being snobbish or selective of friends.

- Failure to admit mistakes.

- Lack of a "teachable" spirit.

- Rebellious attitude toward authorities.

- Proud or callous countenance.

- Self-centered conversation.

- Blasphemous or boastful conversation.

- Intolerance toward other's mistakes.

- "Bossy" – lordship attitude.

TRANSFORMED
by the
RENEWING of your MIND

"YE HAVE
HEARD THAT
IT WAS
SAID . . .

. . . BUT I
SAY
UNTO
YOU."

Overcoming Pride

(chart 10)

BASIC TEACHING
on

Humility vs Pride

BIBLE SEARCH
on
Pride and Humility

1. What is the first of six things that the Lord hates, the first of seven that are an abomination unto him?
    (See Prov. 6:16,17)

    proud look

2. Who will the Lord "not suffer" (or "put-up with")?
    (See Psalm 101:5)

    He with a proud heart

3. According to *Proverbs 16:5*, who is an abomination to the Lord?

    Those proud in heart

    (Look up "abomination" in the dictionary and write out the definition.)

    _____

    _____

    _____

4. What does the fear of the Lord teach us to hate?
    (See Prov. 8:13)

    evil   _arrogancy_   _evil way_
    pride   _froward mouth_

5. According to James 4:6, what does God do to the proud?

    resists

    What does he give to the humble? _grace_

6. From *I Samuel 15:23* fill in the following equations:

Rebellion = *witchcraft*

Stubbornness = *sin and idolatry* ☐

7. Write out *Proverbs 16:18,19* in your own words.

_____
_____
_____
_____
_____
_____
_____
_____
_____
_____
_____
_____ ☐

8. What are the three root sins of the world?
   (See I John 2:16)
   1 *lust of the flesh*
   2 *lust of the eyes*
   3 *pride of life* ☐

9. According to Proverbs 21:4, what is sin?

A high look _____ proud heart

plowing of the wicked □

10. What are some of the results of pride?

(Prov. 28:25) strife □

(Prov. 16:18) destruction □

(Prov. 11:2) shame □

(Prov. 13:10) contention □

(Prov. 29:23) bring man low □

11. Write out *Psalm 138:6*.

Though the Lord be high, yet hath he
respect unto the lowly : but the proud
he knoweth afar off. □

12. Write out *I Corinthians 3:18*.

Let no man deceive himself. If any
man among you seemeth to be wise in
this world, let him become a fool, that
he may be wise. □

page 46

13. Write out *Philippians 2:3*.

Let nothing be done through strife
or vainglory; but in lowliness of
mind let each esteem other better
than themselves.

14. What is the end result of a man who trusts in himself and in his own strength?   (See Jeremiah 17:5,6)

Cursed. Won't see when
good comes, will live in
parched places of the
wilderness, and in
uninhabited salt land.

Draw a sketch representing this man. □

15. What is the end result of a man who trusts God?   (See Jeremiah 17:7,8)

Blessed. Will be as a
tree planted by water.
Won't see heat coming. Won't
quit yielding fruit.

Draw a sketch representing this man. □

JESUS CHRIST

ANTI CHRIST

SPIRIT OF HUMILITY
SPIRIT OF OBEDIENCE
SPIRIT OF SUBMISSION
SPIRIT OF LOWLINESS
SPIRIT OF MEEKNESS

SPIRIT OF PRIDE
SPIRIT OF LAWLESSNESS
SPIRIT OF REBELLION
SPIRIT OF CONCEIT
SPIRIT OF SELFISHNESS

"Let nothing be done through strife or vainglory; but in lowliness of mind let each esteem other better than themselves. Look not every man on his own things, but every man also on the things of others.

Let this mind be in you, which was also in Christ Jesus: Who, being in the form of God, thought it not robbery to be equal with God: But made himself of no reputation, and took upon him the form of a servant, and was made in the likeness of men:

And being found in fashion as a man, he humbled himself, and became obedient unto death, even the death of the cross.

Wherefore God also hath highly exalted him, and given him a name which is above every name:

That at the name of Jesus every knee should bow, of things in heaven, and things in earth, and things under the earth:

And that every tongue should confess that Jesus Christ is Lord, to the glory of God the Father."

Philippians 2:3-11
☐

"How art thou fallen from heaven, O Lucifer, son of the morning! how art thou cut down to the ground which didst weaken the nations!

For thou hast said in thine heart, I will ascend into heaven, I will exalt my throne above the stars of God: I will sit also upon the mount of the congregation, in the sides of the north: I will ascend above the heights of the clouds; I will be like the most High.

Yet thou shalt be brought down to hell, to the sides of the pit.

They that see thee shall narrowly look upon thee, and consider thee, saying, Is this the man that made the earth to tremble, that did shake kingdoms; That made the world as a wilderness, and destroyed the cities thereof; that opened not the house of his prisoners?

All the kings of the nations, even all of them, lie in glory every one in his own house.

But thou art cast out of thy grave like an abominable branch, and as the raiment of those that are slain, thrust through with a sword, that go down to the stones of the pit; as a carcase trodden under feet."

☐ Isaiah 14:12-19

STEPS OF ACTION

How to Overcome Pride

1 **Commit** yourself to Jesus Christ as the Lord and Master of every area of your life. ☐

2 Learn to **submit** yourself to every authority which God has placed in your life. ☐

3 **Change** your sinful behavior. ☐

4 **Begin serving** others. ☐

What is My Be-Attitude?

"But that on the good ground are they which in an honest and good heart, having heard the word, keep it, and bring forth fruit with patience."

Luke 8:15

Write below your honest feelings toward yourself as to your own personal attitude in this root problem area. What do you feel to be your attitude toward this root area?

MY PRESENT ATTITUDE: _____

_____

_____

_____

_____

_____

_____

_____

_____

_____

_____

ACTION I AM GOING TO TAKE: _____

_____

_____

_____

_____

_____

PRACTICAL TOOLS IN MAINTAINING VICTORY OVER PRIDE

1. Draw up a **CHAIN of COMMAND** chart of the authorities over you in your life. Then begin to submit yourself in practical ways to them.

2. Make up a list of the things you possess (materially, naturally, mentally) and after each item, write, "Jesus is Lord".

3. Do further TOPICAL STUDIES from scripture on topics such as: Humility, Obedience, Submission, Rebellion, Authority, etc. (Keep these in a special notebook)

4. Memorize some of the key Scriptures on Pride, such as:

        ✔ Proverbs 16:18,19
        ✔ Romans 13:1-5
        ✔ Philippians 2:1-11

5. Humble yourself by going to certain authorities in your life, whom you may have resisted in the past — confess your weakness, ask for their help and become accountable to them.

GOD'S NEW MAN
A Humble Attitude

"Put off the OLD MAN . . . put on the NEW MAN . . ."
Col. 3:9,10

"Like a tree . . . planted by the rivers of waters"
Psalm 1

"Blessed are the poor in spirit for their's is the kingdom of Heaven."
Matthew 5:3

ROOT 2 AREA

DEVELOPING A TRUSTING ATTITUDE

Overcoming Anger

*"He that is slow to anger is better than the mighty;
and he that ruleth his spirit than he that taketh a city."*
Proverbs 16:32

THE ROOT PROBLEM OF THE WORLD

Because of man's basic sinful nature, he tends to react to life situations in selfish anger when his rights are violated or when something keeps him from fulfilling his selfish desires. THIS IS THE ROOT OF MURDER AND WAR.

PRACTICAL EVIDENCES OF THE ROOT OF ANGER:

- Temper tantrums (at any age).

- Angry reaction to unfairness.

- Expressed frustration over unchangeable circumstances.

- Grumbling, murmuring and complaining.

- An ungrateful spirit.

- Extreme sensitivity and touchiness.

TRANSFORMED
by the
RENEWING of your MIND

"YE HAVE
HEARD THAT
IT WAS
SAID . . .

. . . BUT I
SAY
UNTO
YOU."

Overcoming Anger

(chart 11)

BASIC TEACHING
on
Meekness vs Anger

BIBLE SEARCH
on
Anger and Meekness

1. **Find the results of anger in the following scriptures:**

(Job 5:2) _kills the foolish man_ ☐

(Prov. 19:19) _suffer punishment_ ☐

(Job 19:29) _punishment of the sword_ ☐

(Prov. 14:17) _deals foolishly_ ☐

(Prov. 29:22) _stirs up strife_ ☐

(James 4:1,2) _wars, fightings, killings_ ☐

_____ ☐

2. According to *Ephesians 2:3,* the children of this world are called the "children of _wrath_". ☐

3. Write out James 1:19,20:

Wherefore, my beloved brethren, let every man be swift to hear, slow to speak, slow to wrath: for the wrath of man worketh not the righteousness of God.

☐

Write verse 20 in your own words:

_____

_____

_____

_____ ☐

4. Write out *Psalm 37:8:*

Cease from anger, and forsake wrath: fret not thyself in any wise to do evil. ☐

5. Write out *Proverbs 22:24, 25:*

Make no friendship with an angry man; and with a furious man thou shalt not go: lest thou learn his ways, and get a snare to thy soul.

_____

_____ ☐

6. Write out *Ecclesiastes 7:9:*

Be not hasty in thy spirit to be angry: for anger resteth in the bosom of fools.

_____ ☐

7. There are two types of people recorded in scripture who hold their anger inside — find out who they are.

(Job 36:13) _Godless in heart_ ☐

(Eccl. 7:9) _Fools_ ☐

8. In some cases in scripture, anger was justified. Find *who* was angry in the verses following, and write out *why* they were angry.

(Mark 3:5) Who? _Jesus_ ☐

Why? _They had hard hearts when Jesus wanted to heal a man on the Sabbath._ ☐

(Exodus 11:8) Who? _Moses_ ☐

Why? _Pharoah would not cooperate with the will of God._ ☐

(Exodus 32:19) Who? _Moses_ ☐

Why? _The people were worshipping idols_ ☐

What then, would you conclude, is the only proper time and place for anger? _____

_____

_____ ☐

9. What are the benefits of not giving in to anger?

(Prov. 14:29) _Great understanding_ ☐

(Prov. 15:1) _Wrath is turned away_ ☐

(Prov. 16:32) _Will be better than the mighty_ ☐

10. Write out *Ephesians 4:26*:

Be ye not angry, and sin not: let not the sun go down on your wrath. ☐

The problem with anger is that it destroys the control one has over his attitude and can easily lead into sin. ☐

STEPS OF ACTION

How to Overcome Anger

1 **Begin** to trust yourself and your life to God. ☐

2 **Confess** your sin of anger for any actions of the past. ☐

3 Learn to **give thanks** for everything that happens in your life. ☐

4 **Learn to yield** to the desires of others and begin serving them. ☐

What is My Be-Attitude?

"But that on the good ground are they which in an honest and good heart, having heard the word, keep it, and bring forth fruit with patience."

Luke 8:15

Write below your honest feelings toward yourself as to your own personal attitude in this root problem area. What do you feel to be your attitude toward this root area?

MY PRESENT ATTITUDE: _____

_____

_____

_____

_____

_____

_____

_____

_____

_____

ACTION I AM GOING TO TAKE: _____

_____

_____

_____

PRACTICAL TOOLS IN MAINTAINING VICTORY OVER ANGER:

1. Make a list of the most frequent situations in which your anger is aroused, and then write out, or draw out, what your response in the future will be.

2. Do a scripture study of some of the great men of God in the Bible and discover how they reacted to frustrating circumstances, etc. (See Joseph, Job, David, Paul, etc.)

3. Memorize some of the key scriptures on anger and learn to speak them often especially under pressure. (Verses like: James 1:19,20; Matthew 5:21-24; Proverb 16:32, etc.)

GOD'S NEW MAN
A Trusting Attitude

"Put off the OLD MAN . . . put on the NEW MAN . . ."
Col. 3:9,10

"Like a tree . . . planted by the
rivers of waters"
Psalm 1

"Blessed are the meek, for
they shall inherit the earth."
Matthew 5:5

ROOT 3 AREA

DEVELOPING A FORGIVING ATTITUDE

Overcoming Bitterness

"And be ye kind one to another, tender-hearted,
forgiving one another, even as God for Christ's sake hath forgiven you."
Eph. 4:32

THE ROOT PROBLEM OF THE WORLD

Because of man's basic sinful, self-centered nature, he is unwilling to humble himself in asking forgiveness for wrongs he has committed. He also finds it difficult to forgive others and thereby harbors resentment and bitterness. He is easily offended and continues to retaliate by offending others. THIS IS THE ROOT OF HATRED AND STRIFE.

PRACTICAL EVIDENCES OF THE ROOT OF BITTERNESS:

- Sad or sorrowful countenance.

- Sarcastic, critical talk.

- Inability to trust others and God.

- Frequent sicknesses.

- Frequent depression and discouragement.

- Critical spirit.

- Fatigue, loss of sleep and tiredness.

TRANSFORMED
by the
RENEWING of your MIND

"YE HAVE
HEARD THAT
IT WAS
SAID . . .

. . . BUT I
SAY
UNTO
YOU."

Overcoming Bitterness

(chart 12)

BASIC TEACHING
on

Forgiveness vs Bitterness

BIBLE SEARCH
on
Bitterness and Forgiveness

1. If we don't forgive others, what will happen to us?
   (see Matt. 6:12,14,15)

   God will not forgive our sins

2. How many times are we to forgive someone?
   (see Matt. 18:21,22)

   seventy X seven

   (see also Luke 17:3,4)

   As often as they sin against us

   What is the point God is trying to get across? In other words, how often do you think we should forgive?

   We are to forgive everyone as many times as they offend us. Our forgiveness is to be unending.

3. What kind of attitude are we to have when praying?
   Write out *Mark 11:25*:

   And when ye stand praying, forgive, if ye have ought against any: that your Father also which is in heaven may forgive you your trespasses.

4. Write out *Matthew 18:7*:

   Woe unto the world because of offences! For it must needs be that offences come; but woe to that man by whom the offence cometh!

How often do you suppose offenses will occur?

It is inevitable that offenses will occur continually in our lives.

5. In order not to be overcome by an "offence", what must we do? (see Rom. 12:21)

Be not overcome of evil, but overcome evil with good.

6. Write out *I Corinthians* 4:12,13:

And labour, working with our own hands; being reviled, we bless; being persecuted, we suffer it; being defamed, we intreat; we are made as the filth of the world, and are the offscouring of all things unto this day.

7. Write out *Ephesians* 4:32:

And be ye kind one to another, tenderhearted, forgiving one another, even as God for Christ's sake hath forgiven you.

Why then are we to forgive others?
Because God forgives us.

And what kind of heart are we to have?
Tenderhearted

8. If we have a quarrel with someone, what 2 things are we to do? (see Col. 3:13)

   1. _Forbear one another_

   2. _Forgive one another_

9. Write out *I Peter 3:9*, and find out what our response is to be when others wrong us:

   Not rendering evil for evil, or railing for railing; but contrariwise blessing; knowing that ye are thereunto called, that ye should inherit a blessing.

10. What kind of attitude are we to have toward our enemies. Write out *Proverbs 25:21,22* and underline the instructions:

   If thine enemy be hungry, give him bread to eat; and if he be thirsty, give him water to drink; for thou shalt heap coals of fire upon his head, and the Lord shall reward thee.

11. Fill in the following chart of RESPONSE based on *Matthew 5:43-45*:

GODLY RESPONSE

Your enemy Someone who is opposing you either deliberately or unknowingly.	Love
People curse you Someone who slanders, gossips, puts you down, makes fun of you, your name or reputation.	Bless
People hate you Bad attitude to you, glares at you, ignores or obviously dislikes you.	Do Good
People use you Mistreats or is nice only for selfish motives, or takes advantage of you & your sincerity.	Prayer
People persecute you Verbally & physically abuse you openly, attempting to discredit you, abuse you, hurt, or even destroy you.	Prayer

12. Write out *Hebrews 12:15*:

Looking diligently lest any man fail of the grace of God; lest any root of bitterness springing up trouble you, and thereby many be defiled.

According to this verse, how will a root of bitterness affect you?
Will be troubled

How will it affect others? Many will be defiled

13. Write out *James 3:14,15:*

But if ye have bitter envying and strife in your hearts, glory not, and lie not against the truth. This wisdom descendeth not from above, but is earthly, sensual and devilish.

According to these verses, what are the three sources of bitterness?

Earthly

Sensual

Devilish

STEPS OF ACTION

How to Overcome Bitterness

1 **Fully forgive** each of those who have offended you.☐

2 **Ask forgiveness** of God and others (where necessary) for any wrong attitudes on your part.☐

3 Recognize that **offenses are inevitable** and be prepared to respond in a godly way.☐

4 Learn to **pray honestly.**☐

What is My Be-Attitude?

"But that on the good ground are they which in an honest and good heart, having heard the word, keep it, and bring forth fruit with patience."

Luke 8:15

Write below your honest feelings toward yourself as to your own personal attitude in this root problem area. What do you feel to be your attitude toward this root area?

MY PRESENT ATTITUDE: _____

_____

_____

_____

_____

_____

_____

_____

_____

_____

_____

ACTION I AM GOING TO TAKE: _____

_____

_____

_____

_____

PRACTICAL TOOLS IN MAINTAINING VICTORY OVER BITTERNESS:

1. Start a **prayer list** and begin praying for those who offend you or hurt you. (Matt. 5:44)

2. Write out a **list of situations** that most often hurt or offend you and prepare a proper response to each situation.

3. Do a Bible study on "offend", offended, offence, offences", etc.

4. **Memorize** key scriptures on FORGIVENESS such as *Matthew 18*.

5. Begin each day with a *prayer for GRACE*. (see Hebrews 4:16; 12:15) (Grace is God's means to overcome bitterness!)

6. Learn to read several of the *PSALMS* each morning. (David was an honest man with a heart after God, and yet many times complained to God about the offences of others toward himself. Find out David's secret and how he overcame bitterness.)

7. Study the *BOOK OF JOB.*
   (If anyone had a "right" to be bitter, it was Job!)

GOD'S NEW MAN
A Forgiving Attitude

"Put off the OLD MAN . . . put on the NEW MAN . . ."
Col. 3:9,10

"Like a tree . . . planted by the
rivers of waters"
Psalm 1

"Blessed are the merciful for
they shall obtain mercy."
Matthew 5:7

ROOT 4 AREA

DEVELOPING A PURE ATTITUDE

Overcoming Immorality

*"Walk in the Spirit, and ye shall not
fulfill the lust of the flesh."*
Gal. 5:16

THE ROOT PROBLEM OF THE WORLD

Because of man's basic sinful nature he tends to follow his natural incli-
nations to fulfill the lusts of his flesh. Man's lower nature (his flesh)
craves sensual fulfillment and satisfaction. He yields to lust not knowing
that it leads to his own destruction. THIS IS THE ROOT OF ADULTERY,
IMMORALITY, AND PERVERSION.

PRACTICAL EVIDENCES OF THE ROOT OF IMPURITY:

- Sensual conversation.

- Reading of impure materials.

- Impure actions toward opposite
  sex.

- Tendency toward fantasy and
  daydreaming.

- Impure habits.

- Suggestive comments.

- Desire for sensual music.

- Sensual dress and appearance.

- Carnal curiosity to "see" things.

- Tendency to enjoy nighttime
  better than daytime.

- Tiredness and slothfulness.

- Frequent depression.

- Avoidance of those in authority.

TRANSFORMED
by the
RENEWING of your MIND

"YE HAVE
HEARD THAT
IT WAS
SAID . . .

. . . BUT I
SAY
UNTO
YOU."

Overcoming Immorality

(chart 13)

BASIC TEACHING
on

Purity vs Immorality

BIBLE SEARCH
on
Immorality and Purity

1. God wants his "New Man" to have a "pure heart".
   Write out the following scriptures and see:

(Matthew 5:8) _Blessed are the pure in heart for they shall see God._

(1 Timothy 1:5) _Now the end of the Commandment is charity out of a pure heart, and of a good conscience, and of faith unfeigned._

(Psalm 24:3,4) _Who shall ascend into the hill of the Lord? or who shall stand in his holy place? He that hath clean hands, and a pure heart; who hath not lifted up his soul unto vanity, nor sworn deceitfully._

(Proverbs 4:23) _Keep thy heart with all diligence; for out of it are the issues of life._

(Proverbs 22:11) _He that loveth pureness of heart, for the grace of his lips the king shall be his friend._

(I Peter 1:22) Seeing ye have purified your souls in obeying the truth through the Spirit unto unfeigned love of the brethren see that ye love one another with a pure heart fervently.

(II Tim. 2:22) Flee also youthful lusts; but follow righteousness, faith, charity, peace, with them that call on the Lord out of a pure heart.

2. Make a list of the things that come out of the heart. (see Matt. 15:19)

Evil thoughts, murders, adulteries, fornications, thefts, false witness, blasphemies.

What do these things do to a man? (see verse 20)

defile

3. What is the heart like without God's influence?
(Write out *Jeremiah 17:9*)

The heart is deceitful above all things, and desperately wicked; who can know it?

4. It is very important for a man to have a change in his heart because...

as a man " _____thinketh_____ " in

his heart _____so_____ is he"

(see Proberbs 23:7a)☐

5. It is also very important for God's "New Man„ to learn to have victory over his flesh (his lower nature). Follow the instructions below and discover how to gain this victory:

• Read *I Corinthians 9:24-27* and write out *verse 27* to discover what the Apostle Paul practiced.

But I keep under my body, and bring it into subjection; lest that by any means, when I have preached to others, I myself should be a castaway. ☐

• What are we not to allow sin to do according to *Romans 6:12?*
Reign in our mortal body ☐

• What dwells in our flesh? (see Romans 7:18)
No good thing ☐

•Write out *Romans 8:1*.

There is therefore now no condemnation to them which are in Christ Jesus, who walk not after the flesh, but after the Spirit.

• How does this verse compare with Galatians 5:16? (make a comment)

If we are in Christ, and walking as he would have us, we will have no problem with our flesh.

• According to Romans 8:5 what do those who are "after the flesh" set their mind on?

The things of the flesh

• What do those who are "after the Spirit" set their mind on?

The things of the Spirit

What are the results? (verse 6)

"carnally minded" = death

"spiritually minded" = life and peace

• Write out *Romans 8:8.*

So then they that are in the flesh cannot please God.

•Read *I Corinthians 6:13-20* and then write out *verse 18.*

Flee fornication. Every sin that
a man doeth is without the
body; but he that committeth
fornication sinneth against his
own body.

• What is our body "for"? (verse 13)

The Lord

• What is our body? (verse 19)

Temple of the Holy Spirit

• What are we to do with our body?

Glorify God

• Write out *Galatians 6:7,8.*

Be not deceived; God is not
mocked; for whatsoever a man
soweth, that shall he also reap. For he
that soweth to his flesh shall of
the flesh reap corruption; but he
that soweth to the Spirit shall
of the Spirit reap life
everlasting.

• What fruit do you get by giving into your "flesh"? (verse 8)

Corruption

• What is the fruit of sowing to the Spirit? (verse 8)

Life Everlasting

• What is the difference between the "old man" and the "new man" in
Ephesians 4:22-24?

"old man" = <u>Corrupt according to the</u>
<u>deceitful lusts</u>

"new man" = <u>after God is created in</u>
<u>righteousness and true holiness</u>

• Read Colossians 3:1-10 and make a list of the things we are to "mortify"
or "put to death" in our bodies:

fornication	anger
uncleanness	wrath
inordinate affection	malice
evil concupiscence	blasphemy
covetousness	filthy communication

• According to I Thessalonians 4:3,4, what is the will of God for us?
<u>Even your sanctification; that ye should</u>
<u>abstain from fornication; that every one of</u>
<u>you should know how to possess his</u>
<u>vessel in sanctification and honour</u>

Read *verse 7* of that chapter.

What has God not called us to? <u>uncleanness</u>

What has God called us to? <u>holiness</u>

• Read *II Timothy 2:19-22*.

What are we to flee?

youthful lusts

What are we to follow after? ▶

_righteousness, faith, charity, peace,
with them that call on the Lord out of
a pure heart_

• Write out the following scriptures:

(Titus 2:11,12)

_For the grace of God that bringeth
salvation hath appeared to all men, teaching
us that, denying ungodliness and worldly
lusts, we should live soberly, righteously,
and godly, in this present world._

(I Peter 2:11)

_Dearly beloved, I beseech you as strangers
and pilgrims, abstain from fleshly
lusts, which war against the soul._

(I Peter 4:2)

_That he no longer should live in the
rest of his time in the flesh to the
lusts of men, but to the will of God._

(II Peter 1:4)

Whereby are given unto us exceeding great and precious promises; that by these ye might be partakers of the divine nature, having escaped the corruption that is in the world through lust.

(I John 2:16,17)

For all that is in the world, the lust of the flesh, and the lust of the eyes, and pride of life, is not of the Father, but is of this world. And the world passeth away, and the lust thereof; but he that doeth the will of God abideth forever.

6. How can a young person cleanse his life? (see Ps. 119:9)

By taking heed thereunto according to thy word.

(see Ps. 119:11)

By hiding thy word in mine heart.

(see Philippians 4:7,8)

Through the peace of God which passeth all understanding. By thinking on things that are true, honest, just, pure, lovely, of good report.

STEPS OF ACTION

How to Overcome Immorality

1 **Cleanse your past** by asking for God's forgiveness. ☐

2 **Repent** and cut off any impure habits or actions. ☐

3 **Avoid situations** that would arouse sensual desires. ☐

4 **Begin to meditate** on scripture and establish godly habit patterns. ☐

5 Learn to **walk in obedience** daily. ☐

6 Become accountable to one in authority. ☐

What is My Be-Attitude?

"But that on the good ground are they which in an honest and good heart, having heard the word, keep it, and bring forth fruit with patience."

Luke 8:15

Write below your honest feelings toward yourself as to your own personal attitude in this root problem area. What do you feel to be your attitude toward this root area?

MY PRESENT ATTITUDE: _____

_____

_____

_____

_____

_____

_____

_____

_____

_____

_____

ACTION I AM GOING TO TAKE: _____

_____

_____

_____

_____

Projects

PRACTICAL TOOLS IN MAINTAINING VICTORY OVER IMMORALITY:

1. **Start a MEDITATION NOTEBOOK** of key scriptures on purity to memorize and study.

   Read and meditate on this constantly.

2. **Confide in an older authority** in your life (parent, pastor, youth worker, Elder, etc.) and establish a relationship of open and honest communication in this area of moral purity. Allow this person to correct and advise you.

3. **Enlarge your reading capacity** for wholesome books based on scripture principles.
   Suggestions: The Bible (of course)
                  Christian biographies
                  Christian teaching books etc.

GOD'S NEW MAN
A Pure Attitude

"Put off the OLD MAN . . . put on the NEW MAN . . ."
Col. 3:9,10

*"Like a tree . . . planted by the
rivers of waters"*
Psalm 1

*"Blessed are the pure in heart
for they shall see God."*
Matthew 5:8

ROOT 5 AREA

DEVELOPING A CLEAR CONSCIENCE

Overcoming Guilt

"And herein do I exercise myself, to have always a conscience
void of offence toward God and toward man".
Acts 24:16

THE ROOT PROBLEM OF THE WORLD

Man's sinful nature leads him into sinful behavior. The result of sinful behavior (or violating God's principles of life) is a sense of guilt in a person's conscience. This guilt can lead either to repentance or further sinful behavior in order to compensate for guilt. THIS IS THE ROOT OF MENTAL ILLNESS, ANXIETY, HYPOCRISY AND FEAR.

PRACTICAL EVIDENCES OF THE ROOT OF GUILT:

- Nervousness

- Fear

- Judgmental attitude

- Depression

- Anxiety

- Lack of concentration

- Limited friends

- Hypocritical attitude

- Overly self-conscious

- Attitude of withdrawal

- Magnified pride

- Low self-image

TRANSFORMED
by the
RENEWING of your MIND

"YE HAVE
HEARD THAT
IT WAS
SAID . . .

. . . BUT I
SAY
UNTO
YOU."

Overcoming Guilt

(chart 14)

BASIC TEACHING
on

A Clear Conscience vs Guilt

BIBLE SEARCH
on
Guilt and a Clear Conscience

1. Why is it so important to have a clear conscience?
   (see I Peter 3:15,16)

   Put these verses in your own words:_____

   _____

   _____

   _____

   _____

   _____ □

2. Write out *Acts 23:1:*

   And Paul, earnestly beholding the council, said, "Men and brethren, I have lived in all good conscience before God until this day."

   _____ □

   In this verse, before *whom* was Paul's conscience completely clear?
   God
   _____ □

3. Why should a person be subject to every authority, even the police?
   (read Romans 13:1-5, and see *verse 5*)

   For ___*wrath*___ sake

   and also for
   ___*Conscience*___ sake. □

4. What is the end result of the "Commandment"?
   (see I Timothy 1:5)

   Charity out of a

   (1) _pure heart_ ☐
   (2) _good conscience_ ☐
   (3) _faith unfeigned_ ☐

5. What are two simple weapons that God wants every Christian to have?
   (see I Timothy 1:19)

   (1) _faith_ ☐
   (2) _a good conscience_ ☐

6. How are we to hold the "mystery of the Faith"?
   (see I Timothy 3:9)

   "In a _pure conscience_ ☐

7. Write out *I Timothy 4:1,2*:

   Now the Spirit speaketh expressly, that in
   the latter times some shall depart from the
   faith, giving heed to seducing spirits, and
   doctrines of devils; speaking lies in
   hypocrisy; having their conscience
   seared with a hot iron. ☐

8. How did Paul serve God?
   (Find the verse that tells you in chapter one of II Timothy)
   Verse 3 --- with a pure conscience ☐

9. Write out Job's confession concerning his conscience in *Job 27:6*:

My righteousness I hold fast, and will not let it go; my heart shall not reproach me so long as I live.

10. Write out *Hebrews 10:22*:

Let us draw near with a true heart in full assurance of faith, having our hearts sprinkled from an evil conscience, and our bodies washed with pure water.

11. According to Hebrews 9:14, what purges our conscience?

The blood of Christ

From what is our conscience purged?

dead works

Why? to serve the living God

12. Write out *Hebrews 13:18*:

Pray for us: for we trust we have a good conscience, in all things willing to live honestly.

13. Write out *Proverbs 28:13:*

He that covereth his sins shall not prosper; but whoso confesseth and forsaketh them shall have mercy.

According to this verse, what are we to do about a guilty conscience?

Confess and forsake the sins

14. According to *I John 3:21,* what is a benefit of having a clear conscience before God?

Our heart condemns us and we have confidence toward God.

STEPS OF ACTION

How to Overcome Guilt

1 Make peace with God. □

2 Make peace with **Man.** □

3 Make peace with **Yourself.** □

What is My Be-Attitude?

"But that on the good ground are they which in an honest and good heart, having heard the word, keep it, and bring forth fruit with patience."

Luke 8:15

Write below your honest feelings toward yourself as to your own personal attitude in this root problem area. What do you feel to be your attitude toward this root area?

MY PRESENT ATTITUDE: _____

_____

_____

_____

_____

_____

_____

_____

_____

_____

_____

ACTION I AM GOING TO TAKE: _____

_____

_____

_____

_____

_____

PRACTICAL TOOLS IN MAINTAINING VICTORY OVER GUILT:

1. **Keep short accounts!** Don't let a day go by when you fail to confess any sin you may have committed or ask forgiveness of someone for any known offence you may have caused. Maintain your clear conscience! (It is *very* valuable!)

2. **Encourage others to be PEACEMAKERS.**
   Once you have gained a clear conscience, share your joy with others and encourage them to gain & maintain a clear conscience also.

3. **Do a Bible Study** on such areas as: "Freedom, condemnation, conviction, forgiveness, grace, mercy", etc.

GOD'S NEW MAN

A Clear Conscience

"Put off the OLD MAN . . . put on the NEW MAN . . ."
Col. 3:9,10

"Like a tree . . . planted by the
rivers of waters"
Psalm 1

"Blessed are the peacemakers for
they shall be called the children of God."
Matthew 5:3

Section Four

THE DO-ACTIONS
The Fruit of Character

FRUIT 1 AREA

DEVELOPING RIGHTEOUSNESS

Through the Word of God

*"Blessed are they which do hunger and thirst after righteousness:
for they shall be filled."*
Matt. 5:6

THE FRUIT OF CHARACTER

When a person's life has been transformed by the Word and Spirit of God and he has gained a clear conscience and is dwelling in Righteousness, he has an intense desire for the Scriptures, the inspired Word of God which then begins to make him into a complete and "perfect" man, restored to the "likeness" and "image" of God. THIS IS THE FRUIT OF RIGHTEOUSNESS.

PRACTICAL EVIDENCES OF A HUNGER FOR GOD'S WORD

- Searching the scripture for answers to life's problem situations.

- Discovering "little gems" in scripture.

- Finding God's direction through reading scripture.

- Using scripture in conversation.

- Basing judgments and decisions on scriptural principles.

- A desire to find out the meanings of scripture passages.

- A desire to establish right relationships based on principles from God's Word.

BASIC TEACHING
on
The Word of God

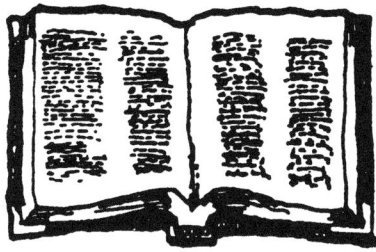

BIBLE SEARCH
on

The Importance of the Word of God

1. The Word of God is alive and active.
   Write out *Hebrews 4:12:*

   For the word of God is quick, and powerful,
   and sharper than any twoedged sword,
   piercing even to the dividing asunder of
   soul and spirit, and of the joints and
   marrow, and is a discerner of the thoughts
   and intents of the heart.

2. The Word of God works in the lives of believers.
   Write out *I Thessalonians 2:13:*

   For this cause also thank we God without
   ceasing, because when ye received the word
   of God which ye heard of us, ye received it
   not as the word of men, but as it is in
   truth, the word of God, which effectually
   worketh also in you that believe.

3. Read *II Timothy 3:16* and fill in the following:

   "All ___scripture___ is given by ___inspiration___

   and is profitable for (1) ___doctrine___

   (2) ___reproof___

   (3) ___correction___

   (4) ___instruction in___

   ___righteousness___"

4. How does faith come? (see Rom. 10:17)

By hearing, and hearing by the word of God.

5. Write out Colossians 3:16:

Let the word of Christ dwell in you richly in all wisdom; teaching and admonishing one another in psalms and hymns and spiritual songs, singing with grace in your hearts to the Lord.

6. What are the scriptures able to do? (see II Timothy 3:15)

To make thee wise unto salvation through faith which is in Christ Jesus.

7. What do scriptures equip the "man of God" for?
(see II Timothy 3:17)

Perfect, thoroughly furnished unto all good works.

8. Read *I Peter 2:2,3* and answer the following questions:

What are we to desire? *the sincere milk of the word*

What will it do for me? *to grow, to taste that the Lord is gracious*

9. Read John 8:31,32 and answer the following questions:

What are we to continue in, if we want to be Christ's disciples?
in His word

What makes us free? *the truth*

10. Read *John 17:17* and answer the following questions:

What "sanctifies" us? *the truth* ☐

What does it mean to "sanctify"? *purge, make pure* ☐

_____ ☐

God's Word = *truth* ☐

11. According to *Acts 17:11*, what were the people called and why?

Called: *more noble* ☐

Why? *They received the word with all* *readiness of mind, and searched* *the scriptures daily.* ☐

12. According to *Acts 20:32*, what is God's Word able to do?

To build us up, and give us an inheritance *among all them who are sanctified.* ☐

13. What has God magnified above His own name? (see Ps. 138:2)

His word ☐

14. Write out *Jeremiah 15:16:*

Thy words were found, and I did eat them; *and thy word was unto me the joy and* *rejoicing of my heart; for I am called by* *thy name, O Lord God of hosts.* ☐

15. Write out *Job 23:12:*

Neither have I gone back from the *commandment of his lips; I have* *esteemed the words of his mouth more* *than my necessary food.* ☐

16. How is man to live? (see Deut. 8:3, also Matt. 4:4)

Man doth not live by bread alone, but by every word that proceedeth out of the mouth of the Lord.

17. Read *Joshua 1:8* and answer the following questions:

    What are we to do with the "book of the law"?

    Meditate therein day and night, that thou mayest observe to do according to all that is written therein.

    What will it produce in our lives?

    Your way shalt be prosperous, and then thou shalt have good success.

    (see Ps. 1)

18. What are we to do with God's Word, according to *Psalm 119:11*?

    Hide it in our hearts

    Why? _that we might not sin against God_

19. In the last days, there will be a great famine. What kind of famine will it be? Read *Amos 8:11-13*.

    A famine of hearing the words of the Lord.

20. What are we to do after we read God's Word?
    (see Matt. 7:24,25; also Luke 11:28; also James 1:22-25)

    Act upon the word, observe it, be a doer of the word, not a hearer only.

Establishing Godly Habit Patterns

IDEAS AND PROJECTS FOR MAINTAINING THE GODLY HABIT OF SEARCHING THE WORD OF GOD:

1. Establish a daily reading schedule. Every christian should read a portion of the Word of God every day. Find a reading chart and stick with it.

2. Take special times to *study the Bible*. There are many ways to study the Word of God. For example:

   (1) Outlining books of the Bible

   (2) Chapter studies

   (3) Word studies

   (4) Character studies

   (5) Theme or topical studies

   (6) Verse studies

   Start a notebook for your Bible Studies and keep your notes in it.

3. Start a filing system for special studies and notes. After completing a study or taking notes, file your notes under the appropriate heading.

   Examples: Topical file

   Book by Book file

4. Start a "Rhema" Notebook or Journal. When God speaks to you specifically about something through His Word, write it down in a Notebook.

5. DEVELOP A SYSTEM for Bible memorization. Start with one section of scripture a month and increase from there. (Also, if interested, there are many publications which present different approaches to Bible memorization. Check with your local Christian bookstore.)

6. CARRY YOUR BIBLE, or a pocket edition with you at all times. Learn to read it during "spare" moments.

7. START A **MARKING SYSTEM** for your Bible. Use certain colors, symbols, etc. This will help in finding references quickly.

What is My Do-Action?

*"Whosoever shall do and teach (these commandments),
the same shall be called great in the
Kingdom of heaven."*

Matthew 5:19

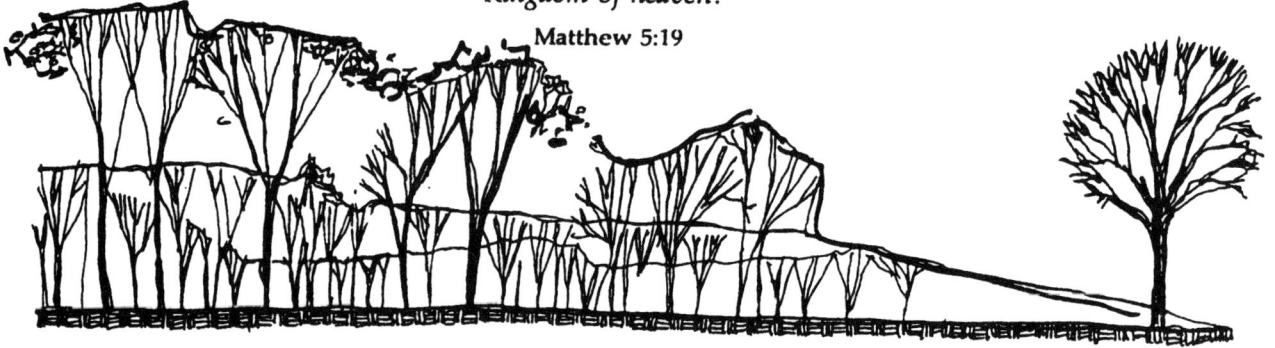

Write below what your present actions are, in regard to this particular area of ACTION, and how you hope to improve:

MY PRESENT ACTIONS:_____

_____

_____

_____

_____

_____

_____

_____

_____

_____

HOW I AM GOING TO IMPROVE:_____

_____

_____

_____

_____

_____

GOD'S NEW MAN

A Hunger for God's Word

"Put off the OLD MAN . . . put on the NEW MAN . . ."
Col. 3:9,10

"Like a tree . . . planted by the rivers of waters"
Psalm 1

"Blessed are they which do hunger and thirst after righteousness for they shall be filled."
Matthew 5:6

FRUIT 2 AREA

DEVELOPING PEACE

Through A Life of Prayer

*"Blessed are they that mourn
for they shall be comforted."*
Matthew 5:4

THE FRUIT OF CHARACTER

When a person has put his trust in Jesus Christ as Saviour and Lord, gained a clear conscience and is dwelling in Righteousness, he has a deep desire to constantly communicate with God. It is a person's calling out on God for grace and help that demonstrates his trust in God. THIS IS THE FRUIT OF PEACE.

PRACTICAL EVIDENCES OF A LIFE OF PRAYER

- An attitude of thanksgiving.

- An attitude of humility and trust in God.

- Ability to pray in all circumstances.

- Ability to communicate openly and honestly with God.

- An attitude of contentment and rest.

- An attitude of security and serenity in the face of adverse circumstances.

- An attitude of joyfulness.

- Openness toward other people.

BASIC TEACHING
on
A Life of Prayer

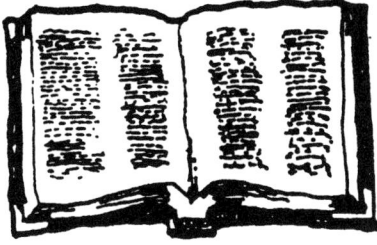

BIBLE SEARCH
on

The Importance of a Life of Prayer

1. A man living in Righteousness has great power available to him when he prays. Write out the following verse in your own words: (James 5:16)

   "The effectual fervent prayer of a righteous man availeth much."

   _____

   _____

   _____

   _____ ☐

2. WHY SHOULD WE PRAY? Write out *Luke 18:1*:

   And he spake a parable to them to this
   end, that men ought always to pray, ☐
   The reason we should pray.
   so as not to faint ☐

3. WHY SHOULD WE PRAY? Write out *the last half of* the verse in *Isa. 56:7*:

   Their burnt offerings and their sacrifices
   shall be accepted upon mine altar; for ☐
   The reason we should pray _shall be called an house of prayer._
   To be joyful in the house ☐
   of prayer.

4. WHY SHOULD WE PRAY? Write out *I Thessalonians 5:17,18*:

Pray without ceasing. In everything give thanks; for this is the will of God in Christ Jesus concerning you.

The reason we should pray: _It's the will of God for us._

5. WHY SHOULD WE PRAY? Write out *Hebrews 4:16*:

Let us therefore come boldly unto the throne of grace, that we may obtain mercy, and find grace to help in time of need.

The reason we should pray: _To obtain mercy, and find grace to help in time of need._

6. WHY SHOULD WE PRAY? Write out *Proverbs 3:6*:

In all thy ways acknowledge him, and he shall direct thy paths.

The reason we should pray: _That he will direct our paths._

7. WHAT SHOULD BE OUR ATTITUDE WHEN PRAYING?
Write out the following scriptures and *underline* the key words that relate to what our attitude should be:

(Job 33:26) He shall pray unto God, and he will be favorable unto him; and he shall see his face with joy; for he will render unto man his righteousness.

(Prov. 10:24) The fear of the wicked, it shall come upon him; but the desire of the righteous shall be granted.

(Prov. 15:8) The sacrifice of the wicked is an abomination to the Lord; but the prayer of the upright is his delight.

(Prov. 15:29) The Lord is far from the wicked; but he heareth the prayer of the righteous.

(Zeph. 2:3) Seek ye the Lord, all ye meek of the earth, which have wrought his judgement; seek righteousness, seek meekness, it may be ye shall be hid in the day of the Lord's anger.

(Mark 11:25) And when ye stand praying, forgive, if ye have ought against any; that your Father also which is in heaven forgive your trespasses.

(John 9:31) Now we know that God heareth not sinners; but if any man be a worshipper of God, and doeth His will, him he heareth.

(I Timothy 2:8) _I will therefore that men pray everywhere, lifting up holy hands, without wrath and doubting._

(Heb. 11:6) _But without faith it is impossible to please him; for he that cometh to God must believe that he is, and that he is a rewarder of them that diligently seek him._

(I John 3:22) _And whatsoever we ask, we receive of him, because we keep his commandments, and do those things that are pleasing in his sight._

8. Jesus was our example. Write out the following:

(Mark 1:35) _And in the morning, rising up a great while before day, he went out, and departed into a solitary place, and there prayed._

(Hebrew 5:7) _Who in the days of his flesh, when he had offered up prayers and supplications with strong crying and tears unto him that was able to save him from death, and was heard in that he feared._

9. When are we to seek the Lord? (see Is. 55:6)

while _he may be found_ ☐

while _he is near_ ☐

10. Write out *Psalm 9:10,12*:

And they that know thy name will put their trust in thee; for thou, Lord, hast not forsaken them that seek thee. When he maketh inquisition for blood, he remembereth them; he forgetteth not the cry of the humble. ☐

11. When should we pray? Write out *Psalm 55:16,17* and underline specific times:

As for me, I will call upon God; and the Lord shall save me. Evening and morning, and at noon, will I pray and cry aloud; and he shall hear my voice. ☐

12. Write out *Psalm 145:18,19*:

The Lord is nigh unto all them that call upon him, to all that call upon him in truth. He will fulfil the desire of them that fear him; he also will hear their cry, and will save them. ☐

13. Write out *Lamentations 3:25*:

The Lord is good unto them that wait for him, to the soul that seeketh him. ☐

14. Read *Matthew 7:7-11* and fill in the following:

Ask, and "_it shall be given you_"

Seek, and "_ye shall find_"

Knock, and "_it shall be opened unto you_"

everyone that asks "_receives_"

everyone who seeks "_finds_"

everyone who knocks "_it shall be opened_"

your Father in heaven will give "_good things_" □
to them that ask him.

15. We should agree together with others when we pray.
Write out *Matthew 18:19,20:*

Again I say unto you, That if two of you shall agree on earth as touching any thing that they shall ask, it shall be done for them of my Father which is in heaven. For where two or three are gathered together in my name, there am I in □ the midst of them.

16. Write out *Matthew 21:22:*

And all things, whatsoever ye shall ask in prayer, believing, ye shall receive. □

17. Write out *Mark 11:24:*

Therefore I say unto you, What things soever ye desire, when ye pray, believe that ye receive them, and ye shall have them. □

18. Write out *John 14:13,14:*

And whatsoever ye shall ask in my name, that will I do, that the Father may be glorified in the Son. If ye shall ask any thing in my name, I will do it.

19. Write out *Romans 8:26*. This tells us to pray when we don't know *what* to pray.

Likewise the Spirit also helpeth our infirm-
ities; for we know not what we should pray
for as we ought; but the Spirit itself maketh
intercession for us with groanings which
cannot be uttered.

20. Part of our spiritual armor is prayer "in the Spirit".

Write out *Ephesians 6:18*:

Praying always with all prayer and
supplication in the Spirit, and watching
thereunto with all perseverance and
supplication for all saints.

21. There are two different ways to pray. Read what Paul says in *I Corinthians 14:15*, and fill in the following:

pray with the Spirit

and

pray with the understanding also.

22. What does prayer in the Spirit ("Holy Ghost") do for us? (see Jude 20)

But ye, beloved, building up yourselves
on your most holy faith, praying in the
Holy Ghost.

23. Write out *I John 5:14,15*:

And this is the confidence that we have in him, that
if we ask anything according to his will, he heareth us;
And if we know that he hear us, whatsoever we ask, we
know that we have the petitions that we desired of him.

24. Write out *II Chronicles 7:14*:

If my people which are called by my name, shall humble themselves, and pray, and seek my face, and turn from their wicked ways; then will I hear from heaven, and will forgive their sin, and will heal their land.

25. What are some different types of prayer?
Read *I Timothy 2:1* and make a list:

1. *Supplications*
2. *Prayers*
3. *Intercessions*
4. *Giving of thanks*

26. What is the *end result* of a life of prayer:
Write out *Philippians 4:6,7* and see:

Be careful for nothing; but in everything by prayer and supplication with thanksgiving let your request be made known unto God. And the peace of God, which passeth all understanding, shall keep your hearts and minds through Christ Jesus.

The end result is *peace in our hearts and minds.*

IDEAS AND PROJECTS FOR MAINTAINING THE GODLY HABIT OF A LIFE OF PRAYER:

1. Set aside a *special time* each morning for a certain period of prayer. This is a good way to begin each day, and establish a *godly habit!*

2. Start a *prayer list* and take special time to pray for specific needs. Divide the requests into areas such as: "personal, family, church, job, friends, ministry, missions, national, etc." Write down the date you begin to pray, the nature of the request and the date it is answered. This can be a real faith builder.

3. Do a *Bible Study* on the prayers of the Bible. You can learn a lot by the example of the Bible's godly men and women.

4. Establish a certain place to pray – a *"Prayer closet"*. Having a special little hideaway for private prayer can be a real help in being open and honest with God.

5. Read Biographies of great men and women of prayer such as: "Praying" Hyde, Rees Howells, George Mueller and others.

What is My Do-Action?

*"Whosoever shall do and teach (these commandments),
the same shall be called great in the
Kingdom of heaven."*

Matthew 5:19

Write below what your present actions are, in regard to this particular area of ACTION, and how you hope to improve:

MY PRESENT ACTIONS:_____

_____

_____

_____

_____

_____

_____

_____

_____

_____

_____

HOW I AM GOING TO IMPROVE:_____

_____

_____

_____

_____

_____

GOD'S NEW MAN
A Life of Prayer

"Put off the OLD MAN . . . put on the NEW MAN . . ."
Col. 3:9,10

"Like a tree . . . planted by the rivers of waters"
Psalm 1

"Blessed are they that mourn for they shall be comforted."
Matthew 5:4

FRUIT 3 AREA

DEVELOPING JOY

Through A Life Witness

*"Blessed are they which are persecuted for righteousness' sake:
for theirs is the kingdom of Heaven. Blessed are ye, when men shall revile you,
and persecute you, and shall say all manner of evil against you falsely,
for my sake. Rejoice, and be exceeding glad."*
Matthew 5:10-12

THE FRUIT OF CHARACTER

When a person has wholly committed his life to Jesus Christ and is living in Righteousness, there is a natural "overflow" of Life which results in a freedom to share the reality of Jesus Christ with others. It becomes a way of Life to be a witness of the life of Jesus. THIS IS THE FRUIT OF JOY.

PRACTICAL EVIDENCES OF A LIFE WITNESS

• A joyful attitude toward life.

• A freedom of expression to others.

• A relaxed attitude around others.

• A desire to share how one can come to personally know Christ.

• An understanding of the Word of God.

• An attitude of trust in God.

• An ability to talk to others about the real issues of life at any time.

• A compassion and sensitivity toward others.

BASIC TEACHING
on

Life Witness

BIBLE SEARCH
on

The Importance of a Life Witness

1. Write out *Proverbs 11:30,* and find the "fruit of the righteous" and what a "wise" man will do:

The fruit of the righteous is a tree of life; and he that winneth souls is wise.

2. Write out *Acts 1:8:*

But ye shall receive power, after that the Holy Ghost is come upon you, and ye shall be witnesses unto me both in Jerusalem, and in all Judea, and in Samaria, and unto the uttermost part of the earth.

What comes before somebody can be a "witness"?

Ye shall receive power, after the Holy Ghost is come.

3. Why did the apostles choose another man to replace Judas after the resurrection of Christ? (see Acts 1:22)

To be a witness with them of the resurrection.

4. How can we overcome Satan? (see Rev. 12:11)

By the blood of the Lamb, and by the word of our testimony, and by not loving our own lives.

5. What attitudes are we to have toward the unsaved? (see Matt. 5:44-48)

Love them, bless them, do good to them, pray for them.

6. What was Jesus' purpose according to *Luke 19:10*?

To seek and to save that which was lost.

7. Write out the "Great Commission" as given in *Matthew 28:19,20*:

Go ye therefore, and teach all nations, baptizing them in the name of the Father, and of the Son, and of the Holy Ghost; teaching them to observe all things whatsoever I have commanded you; and lo, I am with you always, even unto the end of the world.

8. What ministry has God given to us? (see II Cor. 5:19,20)

The ministry of reconciliation.

What does this mean? (use a dictionary if necessary)

To be a messenger or ambassador for Christ.

9. We are to be like Jesus. Write out *Matthew 20:28*, and see what Jesus' ministry was:

Even as the Son of man came not to be ministered unto, but to minister, and to give his life a ransom for many.

10. Who are we to live for? (see II Cor. 5:15)

For him who died and rose again on our behalf.

11. What 2 things, described in *Matthew 5:13-16*, are we to be like?

    1. _The salt of the earth_ □
    2. _The light of the world_ □

    Write out verse 16 _Let your light so shine before
    men, that they may see your good works,
    and glorify your Father which is in
    heaven._ □

12. According to Philippians 2:16, what are we to "hold forth"?

    The word of life □

13. *I John 1:1-3* tells us how we should live the Life we have found in Jesus.
    Write these verses below:

    _That which was from the beginning, which
    we have heard, which we have seen with our
    eyes, which we have looked upon, and our hands have
    handled, of the Word of life; for the life was manifested,
    and we have seen it, and bear witness, and shew unto
    you that eternal life, which was with the Father, and
    was manifested unto us; that which we have seen and
    heard declare we unto you, that ye also may have fellow-
    ship with us; and truly our fellowship is with the_ □
    Father, and with his Son, Jesus Christ.

14. How can the communication of your faith become more powerful?
    (see Philemon 6)

    "by _the acknowledging of every good thing
    which is in you in Christ Jesus._ □

page 152

15. In *Romans 1:15*, what does Paul say about being "ready" to preach the gospel?

    So, as much as in me is, I am ready to preach the gospel to you that are at Rome also. ☐

16. Write out *I Peter 3:15,16:*

    But sanctify the Lord God in your hearts; and be ready always to give an answer to every man that asketh you a reason of the hope that is in you with meekness and fear; having a good conscience; that, whereas they speak evil of you, as of evildoers, they may be ashamed that falsely accuse your good conversation in Christ. ☐

17. Write out *Luke 6:22,23:*

    Blessed are ye, when men shall hate you, and when they shall separate you from their company, and shall reproach you, and cast out your name as evil, for the Son of man's sake. Rejoice ye in that day, and leap for joy; for, behold, your reward is great in heaven; for in like manner did their fathers unto the prophets. ☐

Remember! REJOICE!

Establishing Godly Habit Patterns

IDEAS AND PROJECTS FOR MAINTAINING THE GODLY HABIT OF BEING A LIFE WITNESS:

1. **Maintain a CLEAR CONSCIENCE** each day in little things. This will give you confidence at all times to be a witness of the Life of Jesus. (see I Peter 1:15,16)

2. **Learn to talk** about the Lord Jesus freely and openly. This should become a habit so as to free you to share the gospel with anyone. (I Cor. 2:2)

3. Do a thorough **BIBLE STUDY** on Evangelism. Work from Matthew to Revelation and study such topics as "Gospel, Salvation, preaching repentance, confession, testimony, witness", etc.

   Faith comes by hearing the Word of God, (Rom. 10:17) and a constant study in this area will build your faith to share with others.

4. **Spend time** with someone who has real faith in this area of being a witness. It will "rub off" on you.

5. Take a **Seminar in Evangelism** and be trained to share your faith (e.g. "The Glad Tidings School of Evangelism", South Lake Tahoe, California).

What is My Do-Action?

*"Whosoever shall do and teach (these commandments),
the same shall be called great in the
Kingdom of heaven."*

Matthew 5:19

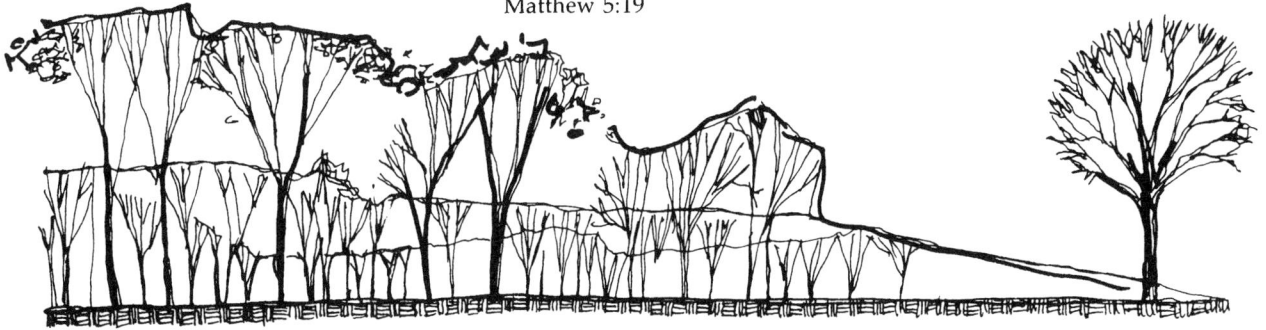

Write below what your present actions are, in regard to this particular area of ACTION, and how you hope to improve:

MY PRESENT ACTIONS:_____

_____

_____

_____

_____

_____

_____

_____

_____

_____

HOW I AM GOING TO IMPROVE:_____

_____

_____

_____

_____

_____

GOD'S NEW MAN
A Hunger for God's Word

"Put off the OLD MAN . . . put on the NEW MAN . . ."
Col. 3:9,10

"Like a tree . . . planted by the
rivers of waters"
Psalm 1

"Blessed are they that are persecuted for
righteousness sake: for their's is the Kingdom of heaven.
Rejoice and be exceeding glad: for great is your reward in heaven."
Matthew 5:10,12

Section Five

RIGHTEOUSNESS
The Tree of Life

What is Righteousness?

DEFINITION:

Righteousness is conformity by faith to the revealed will of God (through the grace of God) and thereby being right in attitudes, right in actions and right in relationships.

*"Seek ye first the Kingdom of God
and his righteousness; and all these things
shall be added unto you."*
Matthew 6:33

BIBLE SEARCH
on
Righteousness

1. In *Isaiah 61:3*, what are those in "Zion" going to be called?

   trees of righteousness ☐

   ("Zion" is the church, and the trees are the believers.)

2. Every part of these righteous "trees" will be fruitful. Write out *Proverbs 12:12*:

   The wicked desireth the net of evil men; but the root of the righteous yieldeth fruit. ☐

   Write out also, *Proverbs 11:28*:

   In the way of righteousness is life; and in the pathway thereof there is no death. ☐

3. These "trees" will be immovable. Write out *Proverbs 12:3*:

   A man shall not be established by wickedness; but the root of the righteous shall not be moved. ☐

4. What is one of the qualities of the Righteous? (see Proverbs 28:1)

They are bold as a lion

Why do you think this is true?

Because righteousness gives a person the inward confidence to be bold and free from inhibitions and fears.

5. Fill in the following verse from *Proverbs 29:2:*

"When the ___righteous___ are in ___authority___, the people ___rejoice___:

but when the wicked beareth rule, the people

___mourn___ □"

6. Write out *Hosea 10:12:*

Sow to yourself in righteousness, reap in mercy; break up your fallow ground; for it is time to seek the Lord, till he come and rain righteousness upon you.

7. How can someone become Righteous? Write out *Romans 10:10* and see.

For with the heart man believeth unto righteousness; and with the mouth confession is made unto salvation.

8. What significant piece of "spiritual armor" are we to wear according to *Ephesians 6:14?*

the breastplate of righteousness □

What area of the body does this piece cover?
And what do you think this symbolizes?

Chest. It protects our heart -- the life of our body and spiritual being, and all our vital organs.

□

9. Look up *I Timothy 6:11* and *II Timothy 2:22* and make a list of things we are to "follow after".

Righteousness   _Patience_
Godliness   _Meekness_
Faith   _Peace_
Love   _Pure heart_ □

10. What four things is the Word of God profitable for, according to *II Timothy 3:16:*

Doctrine □   _Reproof_ □
Instruction in Righteousness □   _Correction_ □

Why are these things necessary?

That the man of God may be perfect, thoroughly furnished unto all good works.

□

11. Although "chastening" or correction and discipline is not always enjoyable, it does produce some good things. What does it produce? (see Hebrews 12:11)

The peaceable fruit of righteousness unto them which are exercised thereby.

12. Fill in the following blanks from *I Peter 3:14*:

"But and if ye suffer for *righteousness*

sake, *happy* are ye . . . "

13. What does the prayer of a Righteous man accomplish? (see James 5:16)

The effectual fervent prayer of a righteous man availeth much.

What kind of prayer? (in your own words)

14. What is the result of the labour of the Righteous? (see Proverbs 10:16)

life

15. What will happen to the "desire" of the Righteous? (see Proverbs 10:24)

The desire of the righteous shall be granted.

16. Write out *Proverbs 10:30:*

    The righteous shall never be removed;
    but the wicked shall not inhabit the
    earth.

17. What is one blessing of being Righteous?
    (see *Proverbs 11:8)*

    Being delivered out of trouble

18. What is the *national* result of Righteousness?
    Write out *Proverbs 14:34:*

    Righteousness exalteth a nation; but
    sin is a reproach to any people.

19. How does your Righteousness affect your parents?
    (see *Proverbs 23:24)*

    The father of the righteous shall greatly rejoice;
    and he that begetteth a wise child shall have
    joy of him.

20. What do we have to look forward to?
    Write out *II Peter 3:13:*

    Nevertheless we, according to his promise,
    look for new heavens and a new earth,
    wherein dwelleth righteousness.

21. What is the work and effect of righteousness?
    Write out *Isaiah 32:17:*

    And the work of righteousness shall be
    peace and the effect of righteousness
    quietness and assurance forever.

Rewards of Righteousness

PHILIPPIANS 1:11   ISAIAH 32:17

The Bible explains that there are many benefits and results from being righteous. List below some of these benefits as they are given to you, or as you find them in scripture.

EMOTIONALLY

PROV. 10:28 – GLADNESS

11:10 – REJOICING

13:24 – PARENTS REJOICE

29:2 – OTHERS REJOICE

29:6 – SINGING

ISAIAH 32:17 – PEACE & QUIET

VERBALLY

PROV. 10:31 – WISDOM

12:6 – DELIVERANCE

SOCIALLY

PROV. 2:21 – DWELL IN LAND

10:7 – MEMORY BLESSED

10:9 – WALK SURE

10:16 – LIFE

10:30 – NEVER REMOVED

14:34 – EXALTS A NATION

15:19 – SIMPLE LIFE

16:12 – AUTHORITY ESTABLISHED

16:13 – AUTHORITIES LOVE YOU

21:21 – LIFE AND HONOR

SPIRITUALLY

PROV. 11:3 – GUIDANCE

11:6 – DELIVERANCE

11:20 – LORD'S DELIGHT

12:2 – OBTAIN FAVOR

14:32 – HOPE IN DEATH

15:9 – GOD'S LOVE

15:29 – GOD HEARS PRAYER

MENTALLY

PROV. 2:7 – WISDOM

3:32 – UNDERSTAND GOD'S SECRETS

12:5 – RIGHT THOUGHTS

28:1 – BOLDNESS

DOMESTICALLY

PROV. 3:33 – HOUSE BLESSED

12:17 – HOUSE STAND

14:11 – HOUSE FLOURISH

11:21 – CHILDREN DELIVERED

13:22 – GRANDCHILDREN INHERITANCE

20:7 – CHILDREN BLESSED

MATERIALLY

PROV. 10:6 – BLESSINGS

10:24 – DESIRES GRANTED

11:18 – REWARD

12:21 – NO EVIL

13:22 – WEALTH OF SINNER

15:6 – MUCH TREASURE

28:10 – GOOD THINGS

God's "New Man" of Righteousness

*"For I say unto you, that except your righteousness
shall exceed the righteousness of the scribes and Pharisees,
ye shall in no case enter into the Kingdom of heaven."*
Matthew 5:20

"Poor in Spirit"

A humble attitude of trust and
submissive dependence on God.

"Meek"

A trusting attitude of giving
to others and not striving
for position or possession.

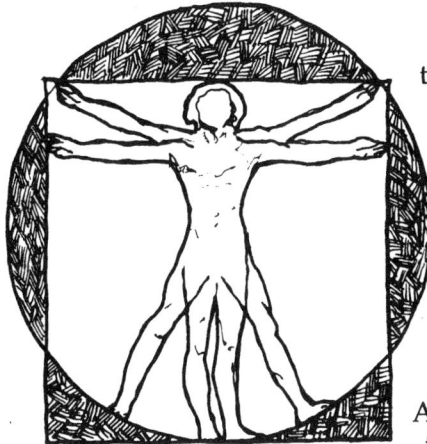

"Merciful"

A forgiving attitude of mercy
toward others and their offences.

"Pure in heart"

A morally pure attitude of
virtue and holiness and
clean thoughts.

"Peacemakers"

An attitude of conscience in which
total peace with God and Man is
experienced through forgiveness,
and others are encouraged to make
"peace".

*"Be ye therefore perfect, even as
your Father which is in Heaven
is perfect."*
Matthew 5:48

"That Mourn"

The Action of being sensitive
to God and pouring out your
heart to Him in prayer.

"That Hunger & Thirst"

The Action of seeking to know God
more and more through the spiritual
impartations of His Word.

"That are Persecuted"

The Action of living a godly life
before all men and sharing that
life with others.

Don't Give Up!

"Don't be deceived, you can't mock God and get away with it! A person's harvest in life will depend completely upon what he sows. If a person sows to his lower nature, his harvest will be the decay and death of his own nature. But if a person sows to the Spirit, he will reap the harvest of eternal Life from the Spirit. And don't grow tired of doing what is right, because you will reap this beautiful harvest in due season, if you don't get weary and give up!"
Galatians 6:7-9

As we continue to "grow in grace and in the knowledge" of the Lord and become more Christ like in character, may we be everything He wants us to be and do everything He wants us to do.

Overhead Transparency Masters

THE ROOTS OF CHARACTER

CHARACTER

A Character Workbook

by Wendell Smith

The Symbolism of the Tree

ACTIONS

The leaves and fruit of the tree represent the *results* of a man's life or his *actions*.

CHARACTER

The trunk of the tree represents a man's *character*.

ATTITUDES

And the roots of the tree represent the *basic attitudes* of a man's life.

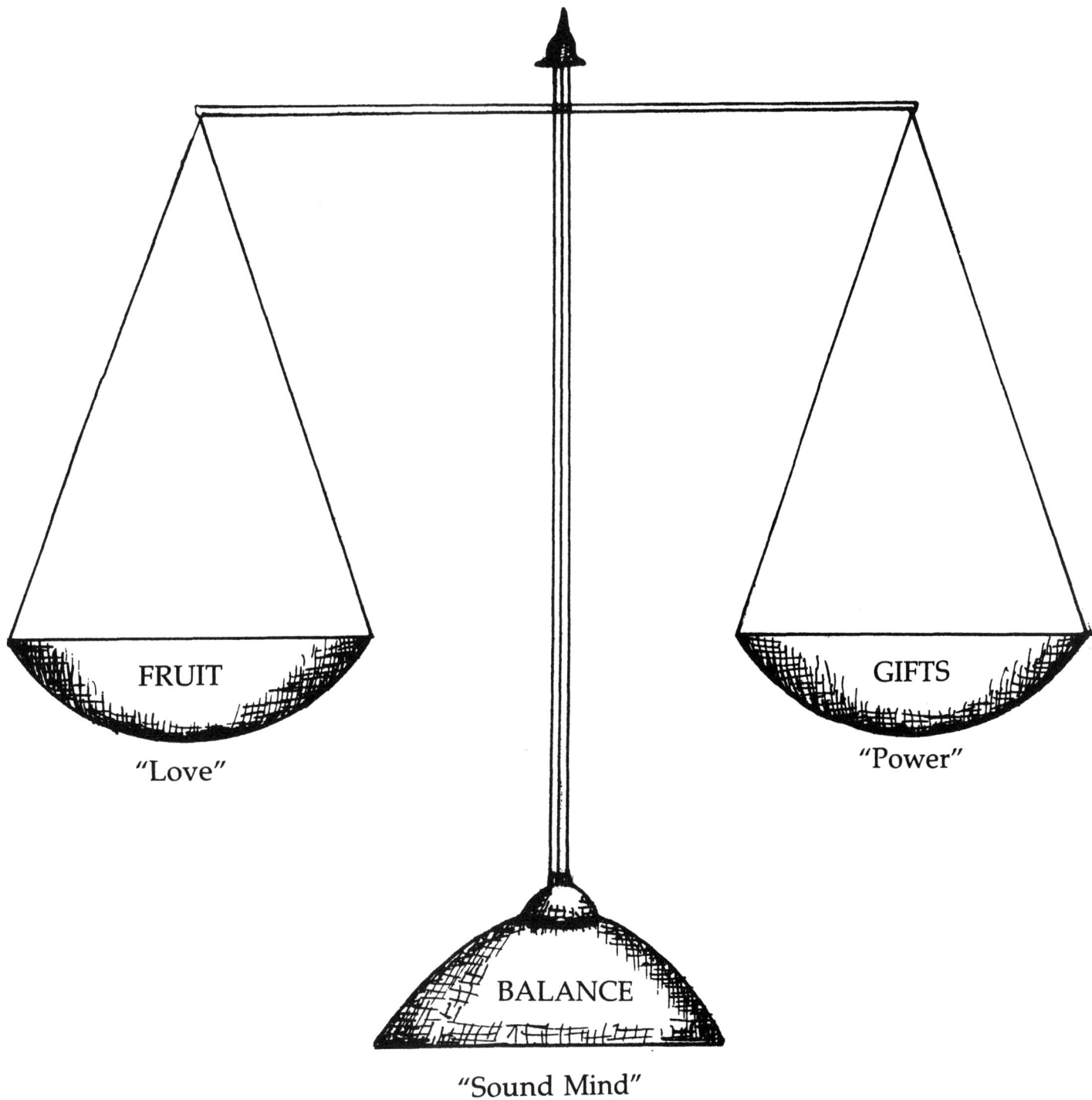

FRUIT

"Love"

GIFTS

"Power"

BALANCE

"Sound Mind"

II Timothy 1:7

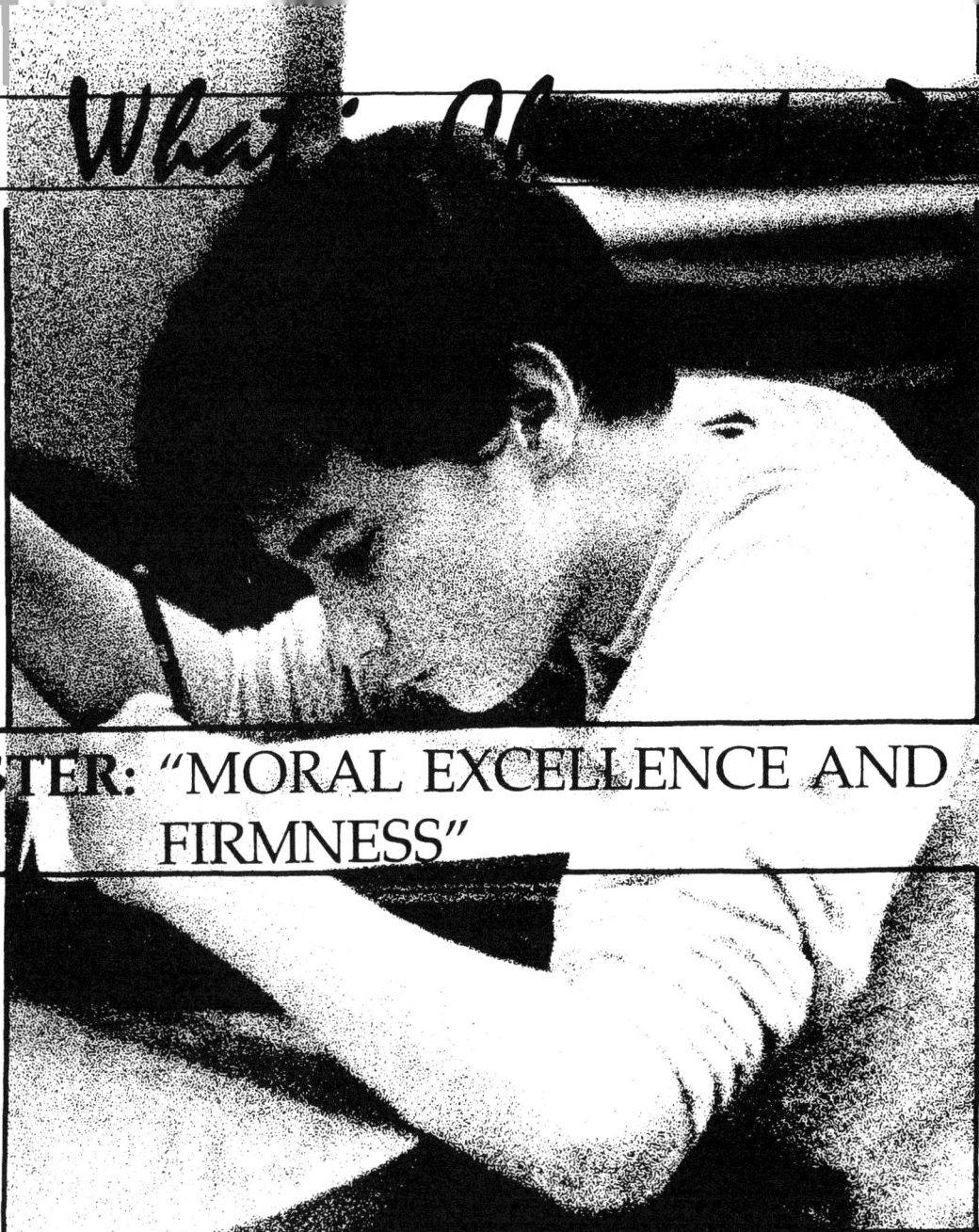

WEBSTER: "MORAL EXCELLENCE AND FIRMNESS"

OTHER: "THE INNER LIFE OF A MAN THAT WILL PRECISELY REFLECT EITHER THE TRAITS OF THE LOWER (SIN) NATURE BEING INFLUENCED BY THE WORLD OR THE TRAITS OF THE HIGHER (DIVINE) NATURE BEING INFLUENCED BY THE WORD OF GOD."

What is Grace?

WEBSTER: "UNMERITED DIVINE ASSISTANCE GIVEN FOR MAN FOR HIS REGENERATION OR SANCTIFICATION."

STRONG'S: "THE DIVINE INFLUENCE UPON THE HEART AND ITS REFLECTION IN THE LIFE."

BILL GOTHARD: "AN ACTIVE FORCE WITHIN US, GIVING US THE DESIRE AND THE POWER TO DO THINGS GOD'S WAY."

GRACE

The God-given DESIRE
and ABILITY to accomplish
God's will!

G od's
R ighteousness
A nd
C orresponding
E nablement

How Character is formed

React

Respond

Developing Spiritual Muscles

As we "fight the good fight of faith" and resist the devil and wage spiritual warfare in our walk with Christ, we will find our spiritual strength increasing as we gain victory after victory. Pressures, stress, problems, hassles, temptations and trials can all work to make us stronger in the "inner man" or stronger in CHARACTER!

Resisting and fighting these pressures is like the pressure of weights against physical muscles which gradually increases one's strength and endurance!

How Character is formed

G

SITUATION

"And be ye not conformed to this world but be ye transformed by the renewing of your mind that ye may prove . . . the will of God."

Romans 12:2

How Character is formed

"I beseech you therefore, brethren, by the mercies of God, that ye present your bodies a living sacrifice, holy acceptable unto God, which is your reasonable service.
Rom. 12:2

RESISTING THE EXTERNAL PRESSURES OF THE WORLD AND ITS CULTURE DEVELOPS INTERNAL STRENGTH OF CHARACTER

Responding to God's Grace

SITUATION	(Man's Way) REACT	(God's Way) RESPOND
SOMEONE OFFENDS YOU	• GET ANGRY (Lose temper, etc.) • GET BITTER • GET EVEN (Revenge, etc.)	• PRAY FOR THEM • FORGIVE THEM • DO GOOD TO THEM • SPEAK TO THEM
FACED WITH A SEEMINGLY IMPOSSIBLE PRESSURE SITUATION	• RUN FROM THE PROBLEM (Escapism . . .) • GIVE UP (Faint) • MURMUR & COMPLAIN • BLAME OTHERS	• PRAY • CONFESS WEAKNESS – ASK FOR HELP • PRAISE AND GIVE THANKS • WAIT
TEMPTED TO SIN	• DWELL ON IT (Thoughts, etc.) • GIVE IN	• PRAY • WORSHIP GOD • READ & QUOTE THE WORD • GET ACTIVE FOR GOD
A CRISIS OCCURS	• HYSTERIA • ATTEMPT TO WORK IT OUT (own strength) • GIVE UP • GET BITTER	• CALL OUT ON GOD • CALL FOR HELP

Being always precedes Doing

AN APPLE TREE WILL
BEAR _____

A WALNUT TREE WILL
BEAR _____

A _____ TREE WILL
BEAR ORANGES.

A _____ TREE
WILL BEAR FIGS.

HOW TO EXCEED IN RIGHTEOUSNESS

(MATT.5)

	THE LAW	THE FULFILLMENT	APPLICATION	BEATTITUDE SCRIPTURE	* OVERCOMING
	"Ye have heard that it was said"	*"But I say unto you . . ."*	*In other words...*	*"Blessed are . . ."*	
1	"THOU SHALT NOT KILL!"	DON'T BE ANGRY!	IF YOU DON'T GET ANGRY — YOU WON'T KILL.	*"Blessed are the meek . . ."*	ANGER
2	"THOU SHALT NOT COMMIT ADULTERY!"	DON'T LUST	IF YOU DON'T LUST YOU WON'T COMMIT ADULTERY.	*"Blessed are the pure in heart . . ."*	MORAL IMPURITY
3	"THOU SHALT NOT FORSWEAR THYSELF"	DON'T SWEAR	IF YOU DON'T TRY TO IMPRESS PEOPLE YOU WON'T BE EXPRESSING PRIDE.	*"Blessed are the poor in spirit . . ."*	PRIDE
4	"AN EYE FOR AN EYE . . .	DON'T RESIST EVIL!	IF YOU DON'T REACT TO PEOPLE YOU WON'T BE TRYING TO GET EVEN.	*"Blessed are the merciful . . ."*	BITTERNESS
5	"HATE THINE ENEMY . . ."	LOVE YOUR ENEMIES	IF YOU ARE WANTING TO DO GOOD TO ALL MEN, YOU CAN'T HATE THEM.	*"Blessed are the peacemakers . . ."*	GUILT

Amplification of Romans 12:2

"Ye have heard that it was said . . ."	"But I say unto you . . ."

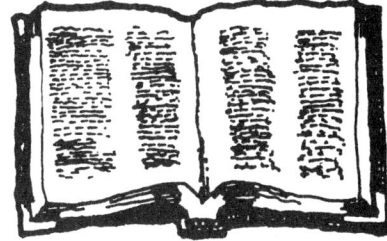

What the world tries to do	**What God does**
CONFORM	TRANSFORM

The BASIC APPEAL is:	The BASIC APPEAL is:
EXTERNAL	INTERNAL

MEANS THE WORLD USES:	MEANS GOD USES:
MEDIA TV, Radio, Newspaper, Magazines, Books *Luke 21:26*	**WORD OF GOD** Teaching (Doctrine) Reproof Correction Training in Righteousness
FASHIONS Clothes, fads, styles *I Cor. 7:31/* *Mt. 6:28-30*	**PRAYER**
ADORNMENTS Make-up, jewelry *I Peter 3:3*	**WORSHIP** Into His Image
MONEY Business, success, stocks *I Tim. 6:6-10* *Mt. 16:26*	**FELLOWSHIP** Iron on Iron
MATERIALISM Possessions, houses, lands *Luke 12:15*	**TRIALS** Fire
PRESTIGE Position, power, fame	**COUNSEL** Wisdom – Evidence
FOOD Food – brands – delicassy *Mt. 7:31*	**AUTHORITY** Covering/Rough Edges
	HOLY SPIRIT Quickening / Supernatural

The Typical Christian Dilemma

TO INCREASE OUR SPIRITUAL
MATURITY WE THINK
WE NEED TO DO MORE
OF THE FOLLOWING:

1. READ YOUR BIBLE!

2. PRAY!

3. WITNESS!

BUT IT IS TRUE...

"YOU CAN NEVER **DO** WHAT
GOD WANTS YOU TO **DO**
UNTIL YOU FIRST **BE** WHAT
HE WANTS YOU TO **BE**!"

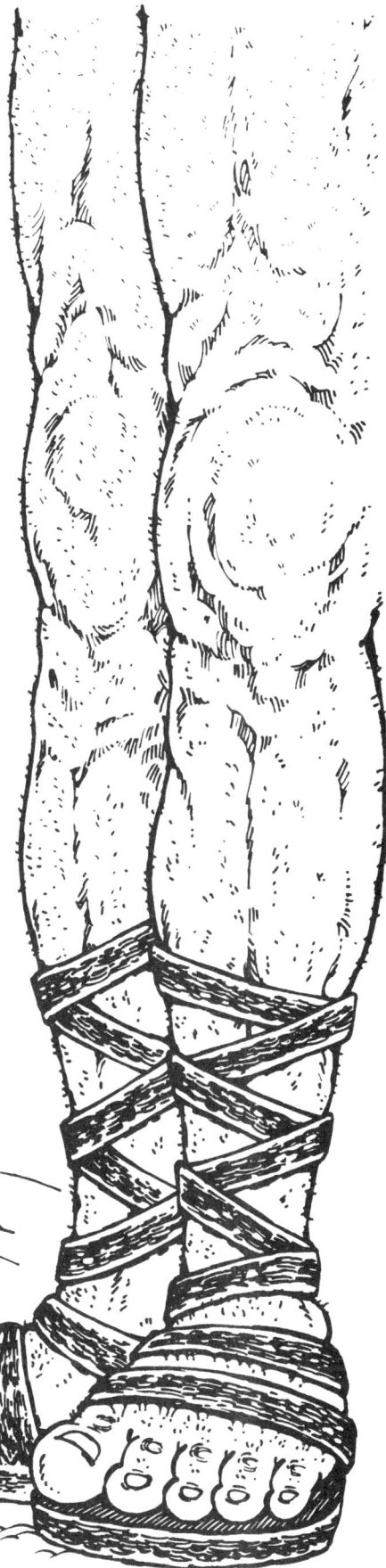

Root Problems in the BE-Attitudes

MATTHEW 5:1-12

"BE" ATTITUDES

	SCRIPTURE	ATTITUDE	MEANING	OPPOSITE Root Problem
1	Blessed are the (those who **are**) POOR IN SPIRIT Mt. 5:3	A HUMBLE ATTITUDE	SUBMISSIVE OBEDIENCE, TRUST AND DEPENDENCE UPON GOD	**PRIDE**
2	Blessed are the (those who **are**) MEEK 5:5	A TRUSTING ATTITUDE	YIELDING TO THE DESIRES OF OTHERS AND NOT STRIVING FOR POSITION OR POSSESSION.	**ANGER**
3	Blessed are the (those who **are**) MERCIFUL 5:7	A FORGIVING ATTITUDE	HAVING MERCY TOWARD OTHERS AND THEIR OFFENSES.	**BITTER-NESS**
4	Blessed are the (those who **are**) PURE IN HEART 5:8	A MORALLY PURE ATTITUDE	VIRTUE AND HOLINESS OF THOUGHTS AND DESIRES.	**MORAL IMPURITY**
5	Blessed are the (those who **are**) PEACEMAKERS 5:9	A CLEAR CONSCIENCE	PEACE OF MIND BEFORE GOD AND MAN	**GUILT**

"DO" ACTIONS

	SCRIPTURE	ACTION	MEANING	OPPOSITE
DO	Blessed are those who HUNGER AND THIRST AFTER RIGHTEOUSNESS 5:6	SEEKING GOD	GETTING TO KNOW GOD THRU HIS WORD	**APATHY**
DO	Blessed are those who MOURN 5:4	SENSITIVITY TO GOD	POURING OUT YOUR HEART TO GOD IN PRAYER	**ANXIETY**
DO GET	Blessed are those who PERSECUTED FOR RIGHTEOUSNESS' SAKE 5:10,11	LIVING FOR GOD	BEING A LIFE WITNESS OF THE REALITY OF JESUS CHRIST.	**FEAR**

TRANSFORMING THE MIND

"SOW A THOUGHT
    . . . REAP AN ACT,
SOW AN ACT
    . . . REAP A HABIT,
SOW A HABIT
    . . . REAP A CHARACTER
SOW A CHARACTER
    . . . REAP A DESTINY!"

The Progression
of
Character

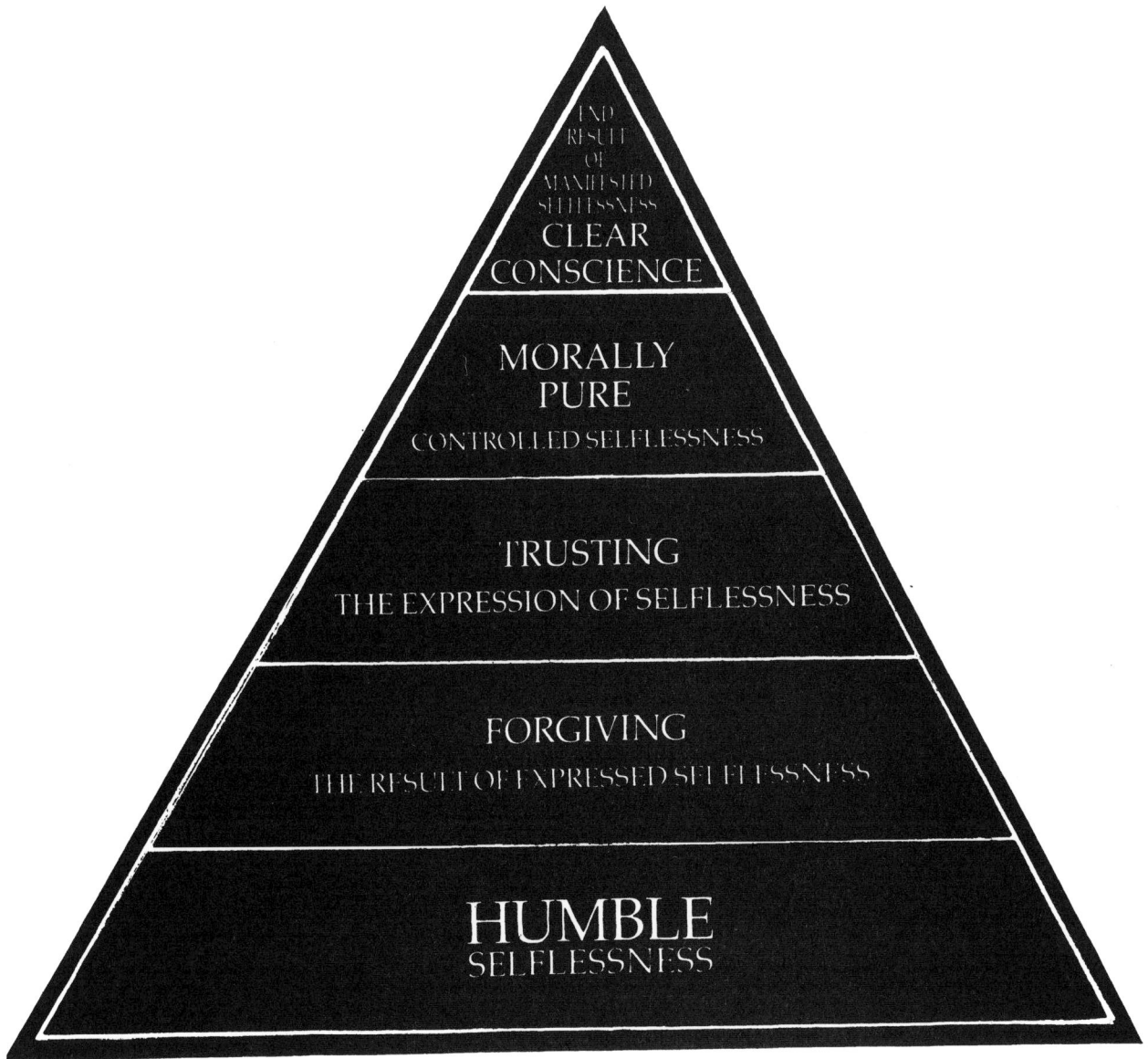

END
RESULT
OF
MANIFESTED
SELFLESSNESS

CLEAR
CONSCIENCE

MORALLY
PURE

CONTROLLED SELFLESSNESS

TRUSTING

THE EXPRESSION OF SELFLESSNESS

FORGIVING

THE RESULT OF EXPRESSED SELFLESSNESS

HUMBLE
SELFLESSNESS

GOD-CENTEREDNESS
as opposed to
SELF-CENTEREDNESS

The Digression of Character

SELF-CENTEREDNESS
as opposed to
GOD-CENTEREDNESS

PRIDE
SELFISHNESS

ANGER
THE EXPRESSION OF SELFISHNESS

BITTERNESS
THE RESULT
OF EXPRESSED SELFISHNESS

MORAL IMPURITY
UNCONTROLLED
SELFISHNESS

GUILT
THE END RE-
SULT OF
MANIFESTED
SELFISH-
NESS

TRANSFORMED
by the
RENEWING of your MIND

"YE HAVE HEARD THAT IT WAS SAID . . .

. . . BUT I SAY UNTO YOU."

Overcoming Pride

PRIDE   VS   HUMILITY

PRIDE	HUMILITY
FREEDOM IS DOING WHAT YOU WANT	FREEDOM IS DOING WHAT GOD WANTS (I Jn. 2:18; Jn. 8:32)
POWER = SUCCESS	POWERLESSNESS = SUCCESS
PUTTING OTHERS DOWN ELEVATES YOU	BUILDING OTHERS UP ELEVATES YOU (Eph. 4:29)
HUMBLING YOURSELF IS A SIGN OF WEAKNESS	SERVING OTHERS IS A SIGN OF STRENGTH (Mt. 3:11)
TELLING OTHERS OF YOUR GREAT DEEDS WILL GAIN RESPECT	GLORIFYING GOD AND TELLING OF HIS GREAT ACTS WILL BRING RESPECT (Ps. 96:2-10)
EXALT YOURSELF AND YOU'LL BE GREAT	HUMBLE YOURSELF AND GOD WILL EXALT YOU (I Pet. 5:5, 6)

4 BASIC STRUCTURES OF GOD'S DELEGATED AUTHORITY

PARENTS

Col. 3:20
Eph. 6:1-3
Prov. 6:20,21
Prov. 30:17
Prov. 15:5

GOVERNMENT

I Pet. 2:13,14
Rom. 13:1-7

CHURCH

I Thess. 5:12,13
Heb. 13:17
I Tim. 5:17,18

EMPLOYER

Col. 3:22-24
I Pet. 2:18
I Tim. 6:1,2

The Purposes of Authority

1. TO PROTECT US AND COVER US.

TO PROTECT US WHILE WE ARE MATURING AND DEVELOPING AGAINST PRESSURES AND TEMPTATIONS AND PROBLEMS WE ARE NOT PREPARED TO HANDLE.

2. TO HELP US DEVELOP CHARACTER.

TO HELP US DEVELOP THE INWARD STRENGTH WE WILL NEED IN LIFE TO RESIST MANY OUTWARD PRESSURES.

3. TO GIVE US GUIDANCE AND WISDOM.

WHEN YOUNG WE NEED THE WISDOM AND COUNSEL OF THOSE WHO HAVE EXPERIENCED LIFE SITUATIONS AND HAVE LEARNED HOW TO RESPOND.

THE KINGDOM OF GOD

THE ACCOMPLISHMENT OF GOD'S WILL
IS DEPENDENT UPON SUBMISSION
CO-OPERATION and OBEDIENCE.

SUBMISSION
THE UNIVERSAL PRINCIPLE

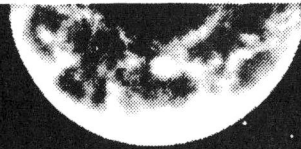

GOD — "Thou shalt have no other gods before me."
– Ex. 20:3

THE STATE — "Let every soul be subject unto higher (authorities) . . ."
– Ro. 13:1

THE HOME — "Submitting yourselves one to another in the fear of God."
– Eph. 5:21

THE CHURCH — "Obey them that have the rule over you and submit yourselves . . ."
Heb. 13:17

THE JOB — "Servant, obey in all things your masters . . ."
– Col. 3:22

THE BIBLE — "Be ye doers of the word and not hearers only . . ."
– James 1:22

MONEY — "Honor the Lord with thy substance . . ."
– Pr. 3:9

PRAYER — "Not my will but thine be done . . ."
– Lk. 22:42

WORSHIP — "O come let us worship and bow down . . ."
– Ps. 95:6

THE DESIRE FOR EQUALITY

"I WILL BE LIKE THE MOST HIGH!"
Is. 14:14

WANT
TO BE

EMPLOYEES = EMPLOYERS

WOMEN = MEN

CHILDREN = PARENTS

MAN WANTS / TO BE GOD

THE
SPIRIT OF *ANTI-CHRIST*

"HE IS ANTI-CHRIST THAT DENIETH THE FATHER AND THE SON – WHOSOEVER DENIETH THE SON, THE SAME HATH NOT THE FATHER."

1 John 2:22,23

THE SPIRIT OF ANTI-CHRIST IS ANY REJECTION OF OR REBELLION AGAINST A DIVINELY ESTABLISHED AUTHORITY OR REPRESENTATIVE OF THAT AUTHORITY

TRANSFORMED
by the
RENEWING of your MIND

"YE HAVE HEARD THAT IT WAS SAID . . .

. . . BUT I SAY UNTO YOU."

Overcoming Anger

ANGER vs MEEKNESS

ANGER

DON'T KILL

ANGER DEMONSTRATES STRENGTH

PEOPLE SHOULD EXPRESS HOW THEY REALLY FEEL

ANGER IS A GOOD RELEASE

IT'S BETTER TO EXPRESS ANGER THAN TO ACTUALLY HURT SOMEONE

MEEKNESS

DON'T GET ANGRY (Mt. 5:22)

ANGER IS A SIGN OF WEAKNESS AND LACK OF CONTROL (Prov. 16:32)

EXPRESSED ANGER CAUSES PROBLEMS (Prov. 29:22)

ANGER BRINGS BONDAGE (II Pet. 2:19)

ANYONE WHO "HATES" IS A MURDERER (I Jn. 3:15; Pr. 17:14)

DEALING WITH ANGER

GOD

ANGER TO GOD
IS **SIN**

OTHERS

ANGER TO OTHERS
IS **SIN**

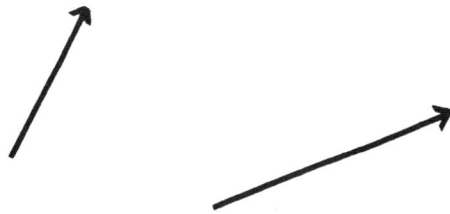

ANGER TO SELF
IS **SIN**

LET ANGER
BECOME AN
INDICATOR OF
A NEED–WORK
ON THE NEED.

CIRCUMSTANCE

"BE YE ANGRY
BUT
SIN NOT!" .
Eph. 4

EXPRESSED ANGER
IS **SIN**

"The wrath of man worketh not the righteousness of God . . ."

James 1:20

MEEKNESS

Trusting God to take care
of my life, my desires, my
possessions, and my rights.

A MEEK MAN

1. Trusts in the power of God to provide, protect, help and change circumstances.

2. Has a divine perspective on life.

3. Is submitted to the will and purpose of God.

4. Has yielded his "rights" to God.

MEEKNESS: Trusting God to take care of my life, my desires, my possessions and my rights.

TRUSTING GOD
TO TAKE CARE OF OUR "RIGHTS"

Developing a "MEEK" attitude
Like Jesus: *"I am meek and lowly of heart . . ."*

GIVE UP

THE RIGHT TO EAT	"Led of the spirit . . . he fasted forty days and . . . nights." *Mt. 4:1,2*	Luke 4:2 Mt. 6:25
THE RIGHT TO SLEEP	"He continued all night in prayer . . ." *Luke 6:12*	Luke 22:40-46 Mt. 26:39-41
THE RIGHT TO PRIVACY	"They have been with me these days . . ." *Mark 8:2*	Jn. 19:23 Jn. 6:3-5 Mt. 14:13
THE RIGHT TO MARRIAGE	"Christ loved the church . . ." *Eph. 5:25-27*	Mt. 22:30 Luke 20:34,35
THE RIGHT TO A HOME	"The son of man hath not where to lay his head . . ." *Mt. 8:20*	Jn. 14:1-8
THE RIGHT TO AN HONORABLE REPUTATION	"Made himself of no reputation." *Phil. 2:7*	Gal. 3:13 Is. 53:3 Jn. 18:30 Heb. 2:9
THE RIGHT TO POSSESSIONS	"They parted my raiment . . ." *Jn. 19:24*	Mk. 15:24 Mt. 27:35 Mt. 4:8-10
THE RIGHT TO LIVE	"Became obedience even unto death . . ." *Phil. 2:8*	Mt. 27:50 Is. 53:7,8 Mk. 15:37 Jn. 10:11 II Cor. 5:15

Yielding My Rights to God

MY RIGHTS
MY WAY
MY WILL
MY POSSESSIONS

TRANSFORMED
by the
RENEWING of your MIND

"YE HAVE
HEARD THAT
IT WAS
SAID . . .

. . . BUT I
SAY
UNTO
YOU."

Overcoming Bitterness

BITTERNESS	VS	FORGIVENESS

"LOVE IS NEVER HAVING TO SAY YOU'RE SORRY"

HATE YOUR ENEMIES

FORGIVENESS IS A SIGN OF WEAKNESS

SOMETIMES, WE HAVE A RIGHT TO BE BITTER

THERE ARE LIMITS TO WHAT WE CAN PUT UP WITH

ASKING FORGIVENESS IS THE BASIS OF A TRUE LOVE RELATIONSHIP (Eph. 4:32)

LOVE YOUR ENEMIES (Mt. 5:43, 44)

FORGIVENESS IS A SIGN OF STRENGTH (Mt. 18:27)

WE ARE TO FORGIVE AS GOD FORGAVE US (Eph. 4:32)

WE ARE TO FORGIVE SEVENTY TIMES SEVEN (Mt. 18:22)

FORGIVENESS

THROUGH GOD'S GRACE

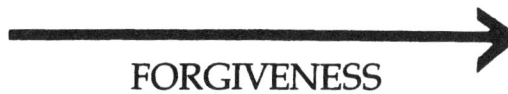

GOD

GRACE

FORGIVENESS

The
BONDAGE OF BITTERNESS

MATTHEW 18:23-35

TRANSFORMED
by the
RENEWING of your MIND

"YE HAVE
HEARD THAT
IT WAS
SAID . . .

. . . BUT I
SAY
UNTO
YOU."

Overcoming Immorality

MORAL IMPURITY	vs	PURITY
SEX IS LOVE		GOD IS LOVE (I John)
GOD GAVE US DESIRES TO FULFILL		GOD GAVE US DESIRES TO CONTROL AND FULFILL WITHIN HIS GUIDELINES (I Thes. 4:3,4)
SEX IS ALRIGHT IF YOU REALLY LOVE ONE ANOTHER		SEXUAL FULFILLMENT IS THE CULMINATION OF A MARRIAGE COVENANT (Heb. 13:4)
SEXUAL FANTASIES ARE ALRIGHT – THEY DON'T HURT ANYONE.		LUST IN THE HEART IS ADULTERY (Mt. 5:27, 28)
THE CREATURE IS TO BE WORSHIPPED		THE CREATOR IS TO BE WORSHIPPED (Rom 1:25)

GOD'S MORAL STANDARDS

BIBLICAL WORD:	PRINCIPLE:	SCRIPTURES:
IDOLATRY	Exalting Someone Above God	I Cor. 6:9,10 Colossians 3:5
LASCIVIOUSNESS	Stirring Up Sensual Desires	Eph. 4:19 I Pet. 4:3
DEFRAUDING	"Using" Someone for Self-Gratification	I Thess. 4:3-6
CONCUPISCENCE	Heavy Physical Involvement	Col. 3:5 I Thess. 4:5 Rom. 7:8
FORNICATION	Sexual Consumation Outside of Marriage	Gal. 5:19 I Cor. 6:18
CALLING	Fulfilling God's Purpose for My Life	Matt. 6:33 Phil. 3:14
EXAMPLE	Demonstrating to Others the Ways of Righteousness	I Tim. 4:12 "Be Thou An Example"

FLEE YOUTHFUL LUSTS

Run from the selfish desires
of your immaturity . . .

BUT FOLLOW AFTER...

1. RIGHTEOUSNESS	Right relationships based on godly actions.
2. FAITH	The revealed will of God and the proper response to it.
3. LOVE	The right attitude toward others – giving to and serving them for their benefit.
4. PEACE	The resulting sense of freedom and satisfaction one has after having overcome temptation through the Grace of God and entered into rest.

OVERCOMING EVIL . . . WITH GOOD . . .

Sowing to the FLESH	Sowing to the SPIRIT
EVIL THOUGHTS	PRAYER
FANTASIES AND THOUGHT PROGRESSIONS	MEDITATION ON GOD'S WORD
SLOTHFULNESS	DILIGENCE AND HARD WORK
BOREDOM AND SELFISHNESS	OBEDIENCE AND SUFFERING
SECRECY	ACCOUNTABILITY COUNSEL
WRONG ACTS	WORSHIP
IMMORAL PLACES	CHURCH ATTENDANCE

TRANSFORMED
by the
RENEWING of your MIND

"YE HAVE HEARD THAT IT WAS SAID . . .

. . . BUT I SAY UNTO YOU."

Overcoming Guilt

GUILT	vs	CLEAR CONSCIENCE
THERE IS NO SUCH THING AS SIN.		VIOLATION OF GOD'S LAW IS SIN (Rom. 5:19-20; Eph 2:1)
WE ARE NOT PERSONALLY RESPONSIBLE FOR OUR ACTIONS		WE ARE MORAL BEINGS WHO CHOOSE TO SIN (Rom. 5:12)
NOT EVERYBODY IS BAD		ALL HAVE SINNED (Rom. 3:23)
WE SHOULD TRY TO LIVE BETTER LIVES		WE DON'T LIVE BY GOOD WORKS BUT BY HIS MERCY (Titus 3:5)
"I'M BETTER THAN MOST PEOPLE!"		EVERY MAN WILL GIVE ACCOUNT OF HIS OWN LIFE (II Cor. 5:10)

CONSCIENCE:

PART OF MAN THAT
IS SENSITIVE TO
TRUTH (or the Will of God)

*"Pressure Gauge" of
the Inner Man*

GUILT:

THE RESULTING
ANGUISH THAT
OCCURS AFTER HAVING
VIOLATED A PRINCIPLE
OF TRUTH

"God's Warning Signal"

THE PROGRESSION OF A GUILTY CONSCIENCE

1. GRIEF and GUILT

2. TROUBLE and ANGUISH and FEAR

3. GUILT-RIDDEN BEHAVIOR

4. RELIGIOUS COMPENSATION

5. VILE BEHAVIOR and ATTITUDE

6. HYPOCRISY and CALLOUSNESS

7. SUICIDE

8. JUDGMENT

Fruit of Character

THE DO-ACTIONS

JOY

PEACE

RIGHTEOUSNESS

PROGRESSION

THE 3
DO-ACTIONS

ACTION	MEANING	FRUIT	COMMUNICATION
"HUNGER AND THIRST AFTER RIGHTEOUSNESS"	DESIRE FOR GOD'S WORD	RIGHTEOUSNESS	GOD SPEAKS TO MAN
"MOURN"	A LIFE OF PRAYER	PEACE	MAN SPEAKS TO GOD
"PERSECUTED FOR RIGHTEOUSNESS SAKE"	BEING A LIFE WITNESS	JOY	MAN SPEAKS TO MAN

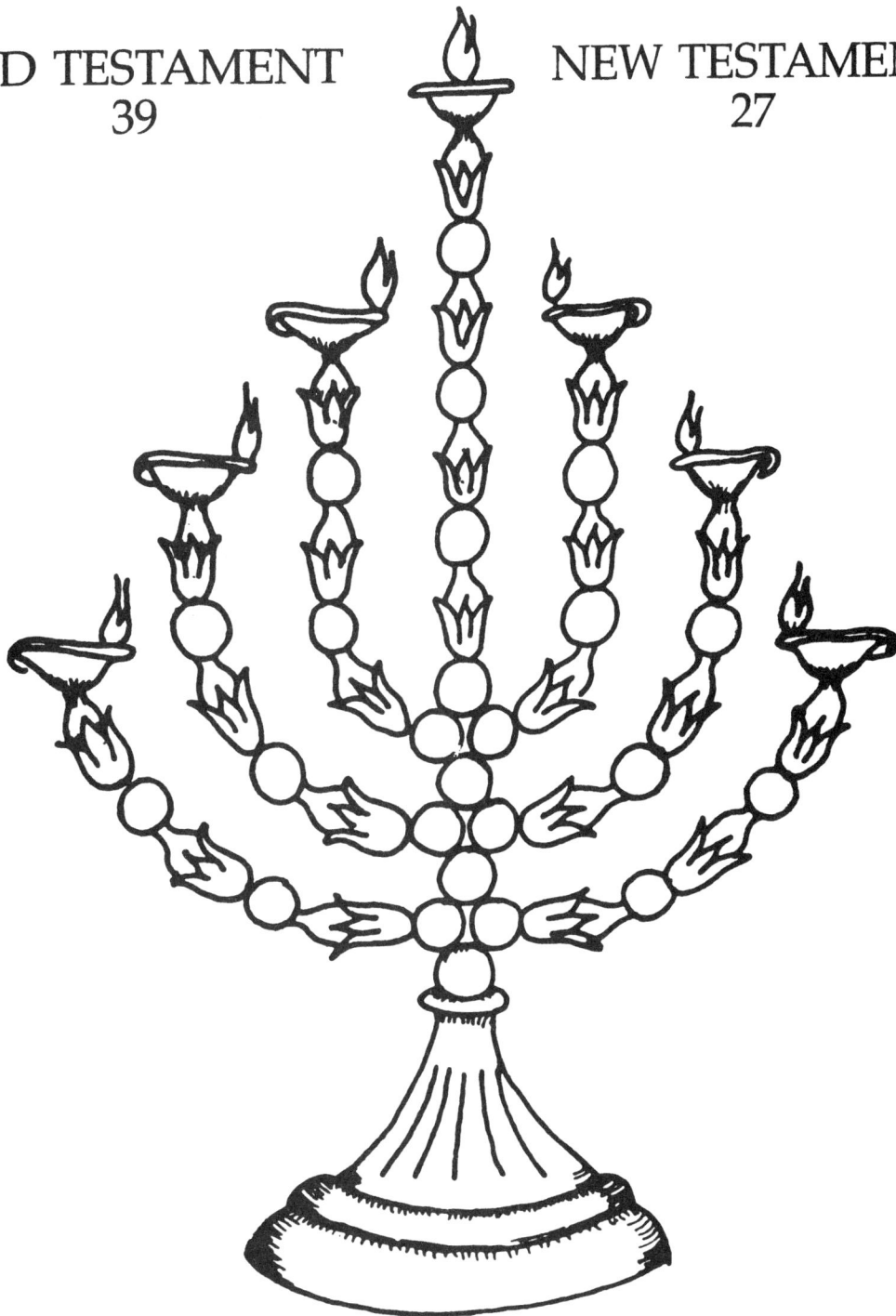

THE REVELATION OF GOD'S WORD

OLD TESTAMENT
39

NEW TESTAMENT
27

"Thy Word is a lamp unto my feet and a light . . ."

Ps. 119:105

WORD OF GOD

Overhead Transparency MASTER

II TIMOTHY 3:16

IS PROFITABLE FOR:

1. DOCTRINE: Systematic TEACHING of God's principles.

2. REPROOF: GUIDANCE and Counsel.

3. CORRECTION: CONVICTION to change.

4. INSTRUCTION: TRAINING for right living. IN RIGHTEOUSNESS

*END RESULT:
"That the man of God may be mature, and completely prepared and equipped for all good works."

3 PRACTICAL WAYS TO USE YOUR BIBLE

I Timothy 4:13

	BIBLE READING	READINGS CHARTS
"READING"	– Public – Family – Individual	Plan Daily Schedule
"EXHORTATION"	DEVOTIONAL MEDITATION	Psalms Proverbs Devotional Material Daily Guidance
"DOCTRINE"	SYSTEMATIC STUDY – Teaching – Individual Study	TOPICAL WORD DOCTRINE BOOK CHAPTER

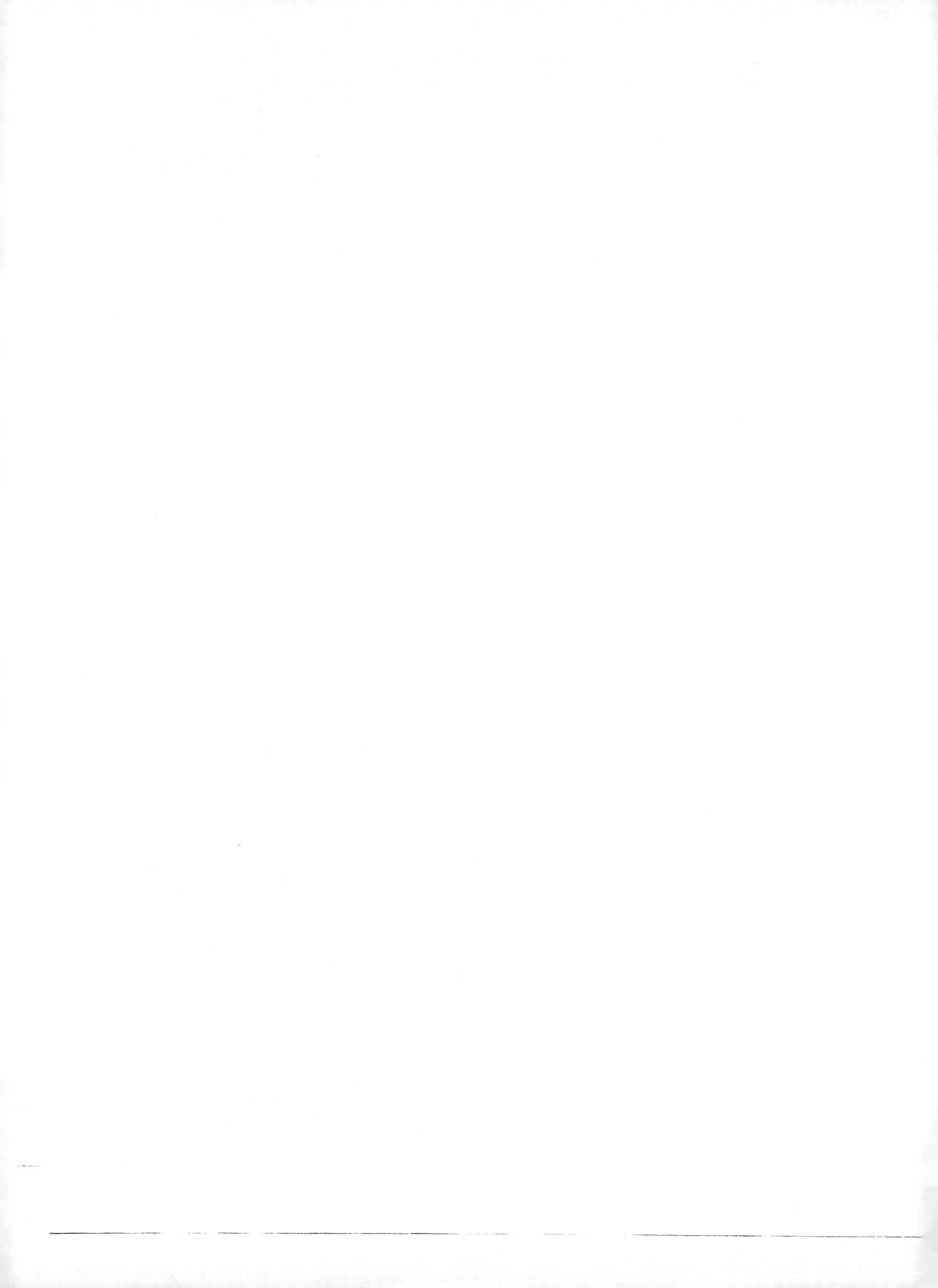

Meditation

1. VISUALIZE

2. MEMORIZE

3. ANALYZE

4. PERSONALIZE

5. HARMONIZE

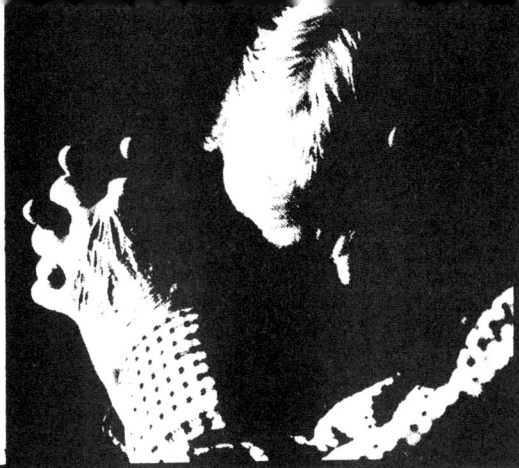

KINDS OF PRAYER

I Timothy 2:1

1 "SUPPLICATION"	PERSISTENT PRAYER	*"to ask earnestly, fervently, humbly – (almost) to beg."* *Lk. 11:5-8 / James 5:16*
2 "PRAYERS"	PETITION PRAYER	*"to make request of a superior – (petition)"* *Phil. 4:6*
3 "INTERCESSION"	PRIESTLY PRAYER	*"to act between 2 parties with a view to reconcile differences (seeking God on behalf of others)"* *e.g. Moses*
4 "GIVING OF THANKS"	PRAISE PRAYER	*"to give freely (offering of thanks)"* *Heb. 13:15*

PRAYER

THE KEY ISSUE IS THE

WILL OF GOD!

1

WAITING ON GOD
DISCERNING HIS WILL

GOD

3

COMMITTING TO GOD
PRAYING ACCORDING
TO GOD'S WILL

2

TRUSTING IN GOD
ALIGNING MY WILL TO HIS

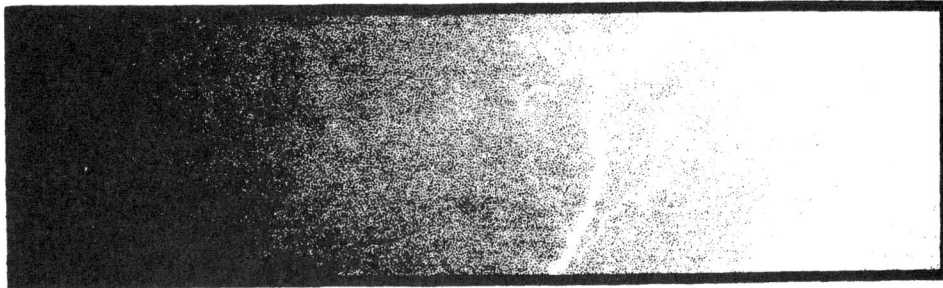

THE PURPOSE OF PRAYER:

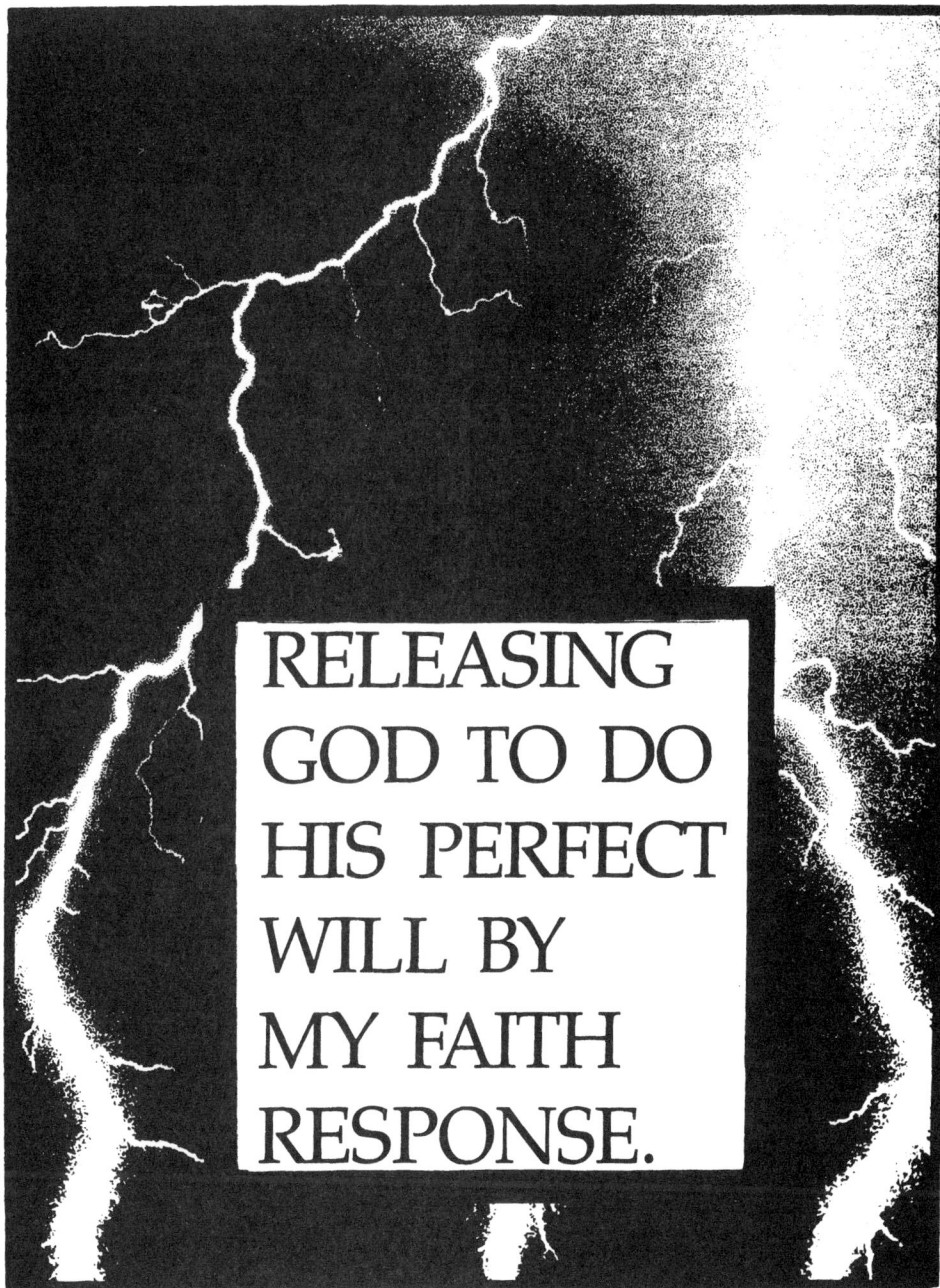

RELEASING
GOD TO DO
HIS PERFECT
WILL BY
MY FAITH
RESPONSE.

6 STEPS TO BUILDING INWARD CONFIDENCE

1. RIGHTEOUSNESS

2. FEAR OF GOD

3. PRAYER

4. ACKNOWLEDGMENT

5. KNOWLEDGE

6. EXPERIENCE

A LIFE WITNESS

2 SOWING
SHARING MY
FAITH IN A VARIETY
OF WAYS

3 PREACHING
PROCLAIMING THE GOOD
NEWS ABOUT JESUS CHRIST

1
A LIVING EXAMPLE
DEMONSTRATING
GOD'S WAY OF LIFE

4 DISCIPLING
REPRODUCING MY
LIFE IN OTHERS

1 EXAMPLE – LIVING DEMONSTRATION

2 SOWING – SHARING

3 PREACHING – PROCLAIMING

4 DISCIPLING – REPRODUCING

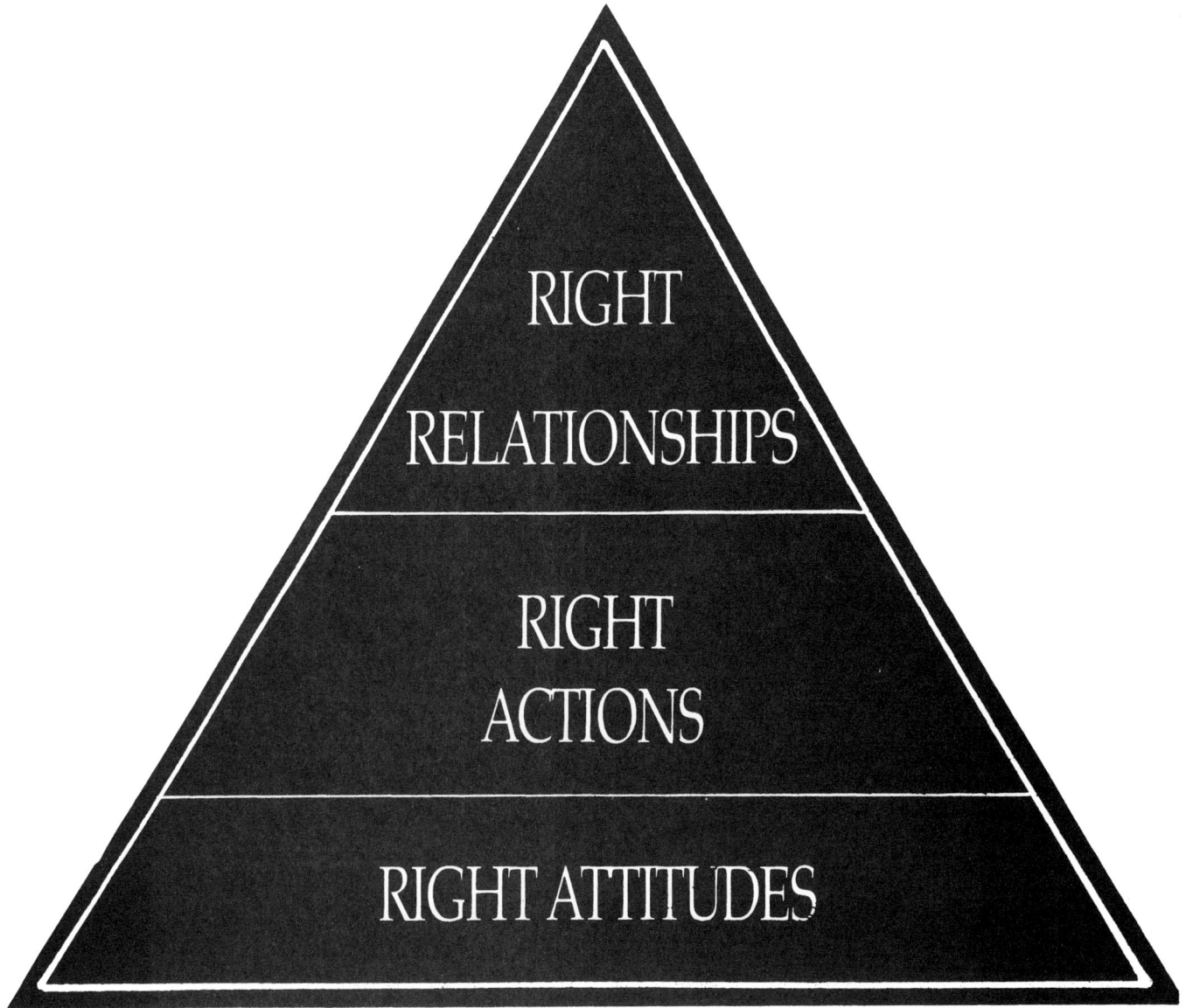

RIGHT
RELATIONSHIPS

RIGHT
ACTIONS

RIGHT ATTITUDES

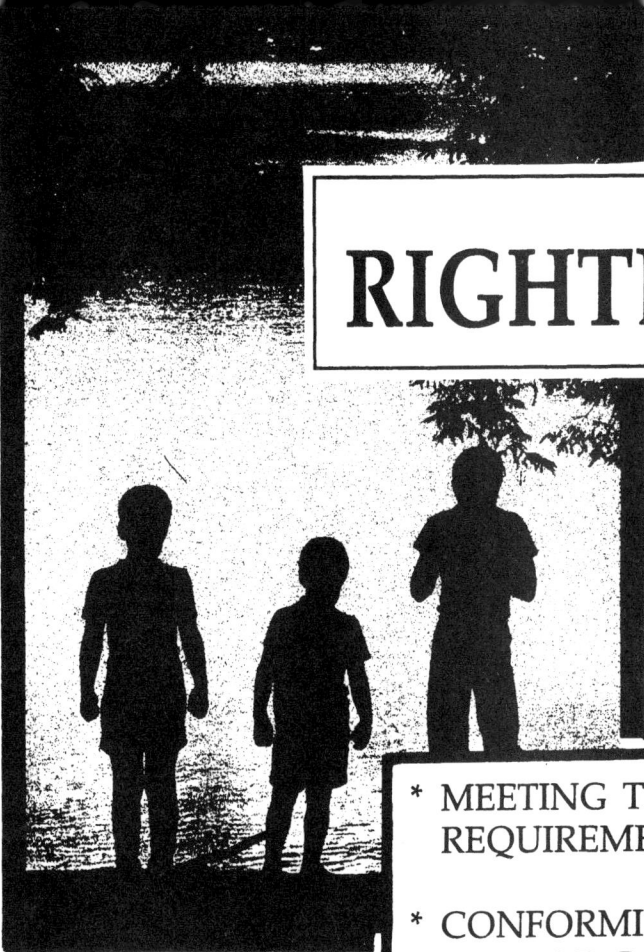

RIGHTEOUSNESS

* MEETING THE SUM TOTAL REQUIREMENTS OF GOD.

* CONFORMITY TO THE REVEALED WILL OF GOD.

* RIGHT STANDING WITH GOD AND MAN.

* THE QUALITY OF BEING RIGHT.

* MEETING THE STANDARD OF TRUTH AND HOLINESS.

* THE QUALITY OF LIFE PRODUCED BY FAITH IN JESUS CHRIST.

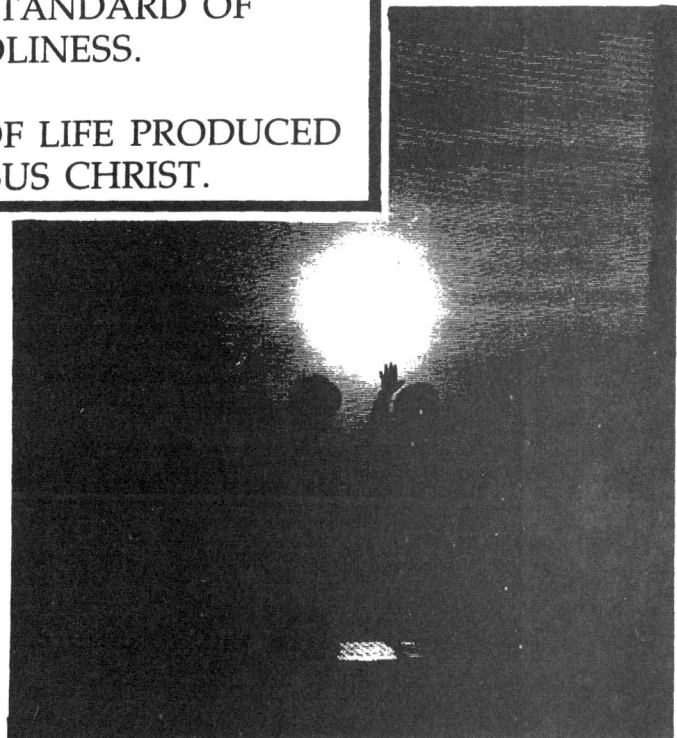